Mission

The *Community Literacy Journal* is an int‹ both scholarly work that contributes to th agendas and work by literacy workers, p cy program staff. We are especially committed t ration between academics and community mem‹...., ‹.g‹....‹‹i›, ‹‹‹ivi›‹›, ‹eachers, and artists.

We understand "community literacy" as including multiple domains for literacy work extending beyond mainstream educational and work institutions. It can be found in programs devoted to adult education, early childhood education, reading initiatives, or work with marginalized populations. It can also be found in more informal, ad hoc projects, including creative writing, graffiti art, protest songwriting, and social media campaigns.

For us, literacy is defined as the realm where attention is paid not just to content or to knowledge but to the symbolic means by which it is represented and used. Thus, literacy refers not just to letters and to text but to other multimodal, technological, and embodied representations, as well. Community literacy is interdisciplinary and intersectional in nature, drawing from rhetoric and composition, communication, literacy studies, English studies, gender studies, race and ethnic studies, environmental studies, critical theory, linguistics, cultural studies, education, and more.

Cover Artist and Art

"Butterfly in a Garden" by Ania Naomi Jones

Ania Naomi Jones is an animal lover, a burgeoning yogi, and a post-graduate student. She aspires to a career in law, in which she can advocate for marginalized populations. She's a chihuahua mom who loves to explore new cities. She currently resides in the Midwest, but is a Southern girl at heart.

Artist's statement: As I walked through the butterfly garden, I was in awe of these delicate and beautiful creatures. So many butterflies were flitting around and I was overwhelmed with trying to get a good photograph. But as I stood still for a moment, a beautiful butterfly landed on a flower just in front of me. I quickly snapped the picture and it wasn't until after I viewed the picture later that I was taken aback by the detail in the image. I'm happy to share this photograph with the journal.

Submissions

Submissions for the Articles section of the journal should clearly demonstrate engagement with community literacy scholarship, particularly scholarship previously published in the Community Literacy Journal. The editors seek work that pushes the field forward in exciting and perhaps unexpected ways. Case studies, qualitative and/ or quantitative research, conceptual articles, etc., ranging from 25-30 manuscript pages, are welcome. If deemed appropriate, we will send the manuscript out to readers for blind review. You can expect a report in approximately 12 weeks.

Community Literacy Journal is committed to inclusive citation practices and encourages authors to cite and acknowledge ideas of BIPOC scholars, activists, and organizers in community literacy.

The *Community Literacy Journal* also welcomes shorter manuscripts (10-15 pages) for three sections reviewed in-house:

Community Literacy Project and Program Profiles will discuss innovative and impactful community-based projects and programs that are grounded in best practices. We encourage community-based practitioners and non-profit staff to submit for this section. Profiles should draw on community literacy scholarship, but they are not expected to have the extended lit reviews that are customary in the articles section of the journal. If you are a community member wanting to submit, and it is your first time writing for an academic journal, we are happy to offer mentorship and answer questions. Pieces co-authored by multiple stakeholders in a project are also welcome.

Please submit using our online submission system. Contact the Project and Program Profiles Editor, Vincent Portillo, with questions at portilvi@bc.edu.

Issues in Community Literacy will offer targeted analysis, reflection, and/or complication of ongoing challenges associated with the work of community literacy. Potential subjects for this section include (but are not limited to): building/sustaining infrastructure, navigating institutional constraints, pursuing community literacy in graduate school, working with vulnerable populations, building ethical relationships, realizing reciprocity, and negotiating conflicts among partners. We imagine this as a space for practitioners to raise critical issues or offer a response to an issue raised in a previous volume of the CLJ.

We encourage community-based practitioners and non-profit staff to submit for this section. If you are a community member wanting to submit, and it is your first time writing for an academic journal, we are happy to offer mentorship and answer questions. Pieces co-authored by multiple stakeholders in a project are also welcome.

Please submit using our online submission system. Contact the Issues in Community Literacy Editor, Michelle LaFrance with questions at mlafran2@gmu.edu.

Coda: Community Writing and Creative Work welcomes submissions of poetry, creative nonfiction, short stories, and multi-genre work on any topics that have ensued from community writing projects. This may be work about community writing projects, and this may be expressed in ways we have yet to imagine. We ask authors to include a personal reflection about the submission itself--information about your community writing group (if you belong to one); your personal journey as a writer; what inspired you to write your piece; and anything else you'd care to share about your life—as an invitation for the author and Coda's readers to consider writing and activism as intertwined. Contact Coda Editors with questions at Coda.Editors@gmail.com.

Authors interested in reviewing for the CLJ should contact Book and New Media Review Editor Jessica Shumake at jessica.shumake@gmail.com.

Advertising

Community Literacy Journal welcomes advertising. The journal is published twice annually, in the Fall and Spring (November and June). Deadlines for advertising are two months prior to publication

Ad Sizes and Pricing

Half page (trim size 5.5 x 4.25): $200
Full page (trim size 5.5 x 8.5): $350
Inside back cover (trim size 5.5 x 8.5): $500
Inside front cover (trim size 5.5 x 8.5): $600

Format

We accept .PDF, .JPG, .TIF or .EPS. All advertising images should be camera-ready and have a resolution of 300 dpi. For more information, please contact the journal co-editors at editorsclj@gmail.com

Copyright © 2024 *Community Literacy Journal*
ISSN 1555-9734

Community Literacy Journal is a member of the Council of Editors of Learned Journals.

Production and distribution managed by Parlor Press.

Publication of the *Community Literacy Journal* is made possible through the generous support of the University Writing Program at the University of Denver. The *CLJ* is a journal of the Coalition for Community Writing. Current issues and archives are available open access at https://digitalcommons.fiu.edu/communityliteracy/

(CELJ)

COMMUNITY LITERACY *journal*

Editors	Isabel Baca, *The University of Texas at El Paso* Veronica House, *University of Denver* Natasha Jones, *Michigan State University*
Acquisitions Editor	Sherita Roundtree, *Towson University*
Issues in Community Literacy Editor	Michelle LaFrance, *George Mason University*
Production Editor and Journal Manager	Walter Lucken IV, *Queens College CUNY*
Book and New Media Review Editor	Jessica Shumake, *University of Notre Dame*
Project Profiles Editor	Vincent Portillo, *Boston College*
Coda: Community Writing and Creative Work Editorial Collective	Chad Seader, *William Penn University* Alison Turner, *ACLS Leading Edge Fellow,* *Jackson, Mississippi* Stephanie Wade, *Stony Brook University*
Senior Copyeditor	Elvira Carrizal-Dukes, *University of Texas at El Paso*
Copyeditors	Walter Lucken IV, *Queens College CUNY* Keshia McClantoc, *University of Nebraska-Lincoln* Marco Navarro, *Queens College CUNY* Cayce Wicks, *Florida International University*

COMMUNITY LITERACY *journal*

Spring 2024
Volume 18, Issue 2

Book and New Media Reviews

Editors' Introduction

Isabel Baca and Natasha Jones

We begin this issue with gratitude and thanks as we are happy to share the 2024 Spring Issue with our readers and welcome Natasha N. Jones of Michigan State University as this issue's journal co-editor. As co-editors who are familiarizing ourselves with the editorial and publishing processes of the *CLJ*, we are grateful to Veronica House for her guidance and mentoring. We are proud of this issue and thank all of our contributors and the entire editorial team. We are also thankful for the strides made in writing studies that encourage our scholars and students to see community as key to making change within and beyond the academy. As co-editors of this issue, we acknowledge that scholarship about community engagement must toe a delicate line between labor and love, between possibility and politics, between research and reciprocity, between representation and remembering, and between pedagogy and promise. The work in this issue of CLJ interrogates some of these ideals by analyzing community engaged work in different physical and temporal spaces.

In this issue, our contributing authors expand our understanding of different types of sites of community literacy, examine the interplay between public memory and countermemory, and interrogate the pedagogical possibilities of combining archival research with reflection in community-based learning. Each of these articles brings to the fore the role of community engagement and pedagogy in a push toward inclusion and local, as well as broader socio political, activist work. The authors of these three articles each ground their work in specific sites of community engagement, highlighting the rich variety of contexts, spaces, and places in which scholars in rhetoric and composition and writing studies can be impactful in their commitment to fostering a deeper understanding of what it means to work with and in communities and progress ideals of equality and justice. We are excited about these three articles and the examples shared within them.

In the first article of this issue, "Mainstreaming Countermemory: Tracing Marginalized Narratives through Media Representations and Community-Engaged Memory Work," Elliott Cochran and April L. O'Brien focus on countermemory shifts and address the reasons for such shifts. More specifically, Cochran and O'Brien examine the role of media portrayals in film and television series and the impact of grassroots community-engaged public memory efforts.Through an analysis of three examples-the life story of Bass Reeves, the Tulsa Race Massacre, and the Freedom Summer Murders – Cochran and O'Brien explain how patterns emerge, and they explore how and why countermemory shifts. The authors examine the broader rhetorical context of shifting public narratives and collective memory and note that community engagement paired with visibility in media can help to illuminate the historical community narratives of Black people in the United States.

Angela Muir, in "'To Open Eyes': Community Literacies, Radical Democracy and a Pedagogy Presence at Black Mountain College, 1933-1957," makes a case for Black Mountain College, in North Carolina, as a community literacy site. Through a description of Black Mountain College's principles and pedagogy with an interdisciplinary approach, Muir argues that rhetoric and composition scholars can expand our understanding of sites of literacy and these sites' roles in engaged democracy and political and pedagogical inclusion. Muir, additionally, discusses how Black Mountain College's approaches to education and pedagogy resulted in antiracist literacies and activism, via what Muir terms, a pedagogy of presence. Muir asks readers to consider the example of Black Mountain College's values as a way forward for understanding different types of literacies and democratic citizenship beyond traditional classroom and curricular practices.

In "Entering the 'Headspace' of Community-Based Archival Research: Reflection and Invention in an Undergraduate Community Literacy Course," Jens Lloyd, through a description of a course that merges archival research and community-based learning and a qualitative study of students' reflections, explores the benefits students gain as community-aware, archival researchers and how such coursework impacts students. Lloyd demonstrates that teacher-scholars can help students build meaningful connections with community organizations even after class projects and university semesters end.

For our **Issues in Community Literacy section**, edited by Michelle LeFrance, we present three pieces, "How Community Means" by Donnie Johnson Sackey, "'Inviting the Body': Walking Methodologies as a Process of Unlearning" by Jamie Crosswhite, and " Identifying a Gap in Prison Literacies: The Needs of Formerly Incarcerated Sexual Offenders" by David Kocik, Casey O'Ceallaigh, Kayla Fetting, and Maria Novotny.

Finally, you'll find our **Book and New Media Review** section, edited by Jessica Shumake. This section includes 2 book reviews: Rosanne Carlo's review of Charles N. Lesh's book, *The Writing of Where: Graffiti and The Production of Writing Spaces* and Patrick Thomas Morgan's review of Wendy S. Hesford's *Violent Exceptions: Children's Human Rights and Humanitarian Rhetorics.*

Articles

Mainstreaming Countermemory: Tracing Marginalized Narratives Through Media Representations and Community-Engaged Memory Work

Elliott Cochran and April L. O'Brien

Abstract

This article seeks to determine how and why countermemory shifts from being a fringe narrative to being a part of the U.S.'s collective narrative. We establish two complementary–and often interlocking–reasons for this shift: 1) The role of media portrayals in film and series, and 2) The impact of grassroots community-engaged public memory efforts. In the examples we study, media portrayals preceded community-engaged memory work, but these findings must be analyzed in context with the community work as part of larger rhetorical ecologies. In our research, it becomes evident that media representations can initially inspire community interest, helping groups organize and craft memory sites to shift narratives within a larger socio-political context.

Keywords: countermemory; public memory; community engagement; Bass Reeves; media

Introduction

Two streaming programs were recently announced that highlight the life and achievements of Bass Reeves, one of the first Black U.S. deputy marshals in United States history. Paramount+'s *Lawman: Bass Reeves* and Amazon's *Twin Territories* signal the potential progression of Reeves's narrative from a celebrated/ symbolic countermemory into mainstream public memory. To date, our collective cultural memory and understanding of the "Wild West," a period between the 1860s and the 1890s, has been heavily influenced by historical accounts and cinematic adaptations that have largely featured white men who were often characterized as outlaws. In contrast, Bass Reeves is the antithesis of this depiction: a Black man and prominent lawman of the period. His existence in juxtaposition to the popularized narrative of the time demonstrates achievements and accomplishments that have largely been erased from popular "Wild West" narratives. Recently, two community-engaged public memory projects to celebrate Reeves' accomplishments have developed in the Southern United States. One in Fort Smith, Arkansas which was completed in 2012 and another in Muskogee, Oklahoma which is still in the planning stages. These monuments frame the beginning of a transitional narrative of Reeves, deceased over 100 years ago, finally beginning to receive recognition in line with his accomplishments. These acts of progress, such as the erecting of monuments, may signal a change. The advancements in unearthing Black public memory figures, such as Reeves, shine light on previously stifled narratives that rebut decades of Hollywood "Wild West" characterizations that systematically erased Black lives. In this article, we critically examine three cases involving Black public figures or events to highlight how the different stages of recognition and acceptance in public memory: The Freedom Summer Murders, The Tulsa Race Massacre, and the life story of Bass Reeves, one of the first Black U.S. deputy marshals in United States history. Throughout the analysis, we determine media portrayals and community-engaged memory work as two causes for "fringe" countermemory to become part of the mainstream public memory.

In the United States, public memory is an ongoing negotiation. More often than not, tensions arise from the debates between citizens and institutions about how historical events, people, and places are communicated in the public sphere. Amy Lueck, Matthew Kroot, and Lee Panich write that "public memory, like all ideological claims about the past, does not merely reflect and preserve, but rather asserts and transmits conceptions of history, culture, and identity" (9). Moreover, Black public memory in the United States has been historically marginalized or outright erased, as have many narratives of Indigenous, Latinx, and AAPI people (Dickinson, Blair, and Ott; Dickinson, Ott, and Aoki; Gruenewald; Loewen; O'Brien "Exclusionary"). The tensions between established historical narratives and marginalized voices that challenge those narratives produce what O'Brien and Sanchez call "countermemory." They contend that countermemories "present a competing narrative of the same evidence, augmenting the narrative already in place with additional information, or telling the story from the perspective of a marginalized group or person" (9). Specifically, countermemory draws attention to the challenges of bringing these competing memories to light, which we can observe in the current debate over teaching K12 students about implications of racism and slavery. As a result, sites and artifacts of countermemory often remain a fringe narrative as opposed to more mainstream public narrative. In this article we trace the rhetorical movement of countermemory as it becomes a part of the larger accepted cultural narrative, rather than simply challenging or confronting a dominant historical narrative.

Extending the work of rhetoric scholars who examine the role of race or racism in public memory (Dickinson, Ott, and Aoki.; Gruenewald; Lueck et al.; O'Brien and Sanchez; Poirot & Watson; Tell), this article seeks to determine how and why countermemory shifts from being a fringe narrative to being a part of the U.S.'s collective narrative. We establish two complementary–and often interlocking–reasons for this shift: 1) The role of media portrayals in film and series, and 2) The impact of grassroots community-engaged public memory efforts. In the examples we study, media portrayals preceded community-engaged memory work, but these findings must be analyzed in context with the community work as part of larger rhetorical ecologies. In our research, it becomes evident that media representations can initially inspire community interest, helping groups organize and craft memory sites to shift narratives within a larger socio-political context via "a circulating ecology of effects, enactments, and events" (Edbauer 9). In other words, it is necessary to recontextualize how rhetoric operates within public memory and observe the fluctuating impacts of these causes. In our analysis, we focus on HBO's 2019 *Watchmen* and the 1988 film, *Mississippi Burning,* because these unflinching depictions resonated with viewers, many of which were previously unaware of these historic events and presented a perspective outside of mainstream public memory. We also highlight the community-engaged memory work in Fort Smith, Arkansas, where residents sought to commemorate Bass Reeves' accomplishments; and in Muskogee, Oklahoma, where community members plan to erect a statue on the grounds of Three Rivers Museum; in Tulsa, Oklahoma. This site is of particular importance because it is the site of where a group of community activists created the 1921 Tulsa Race Massacre Centennial Commission. And lastly, in Philadelphia, Mississippi, where Black community members remember the "Freedom Summer Murders" each year through an annual memorial service. As such, these historic figures and events take their rightful place in public memory rather than remaining as countermemories, or an interpretive account. Ultimately, we consider to what extent these examples speak to a larger evolution for countermemory and what Gruenewald calls the "transformative potential for enacting justice" (5).

Background

We focus on three major examples in this article. These examples illustrate a variety of individuals in space and time similar in that each depicts Black public memory previously overlooked in our cultural public memory prior to their on-screen historic depictions. The Tulsa Race Massacre and the Freedom Summer murders represent racialized violence and death of Black men, women, and children and even white individuals in an attempt to stifle Civil Rights. Whereas Reeves' story does not involve violence, his existence and mastery of his craft in the period exhibits continued repression from mainstream public memory. We provide a brief background of each example:

- Bass Reeves: Born into slavery in 1838, Reeves would later serve as one of the first Black U.S. deputy marshals west of the Mississippi. Reeves achieved legendary status as a lawman and was nicknamed "invincible marshal" (Burton 18) over the course of 30 years of service which resulted in the arrest of over 3,000 outlaws across Indian Territory and pre-statehood Oklahoma, home to several Indian nations living in the area, including the Apache, Arapaho, Comanche, Kiowa, Osage and Wichita (McKay).
- The Tulsa Race Massacre: The Tulsa Race Massacre took place on June 1, 1921. During the ordeal more than 1,200 buildings, including homes, churches, schools, and businesses, were burned and destroyed by a group of 1,000 white people who stormed the Greenwood District, often referred to as

"Black Wall Street." The aftermath left 10,000 Black residents homeless, while somewhere between 100 and 300 people lost their lives ("Tulsa's Historic").
- Freedom Summer Murders: Three civil rights activists, Michael Schwerner, 24, James Chaney, 21, and Andrew Goodman, 20 were brutally murdered and buried in the small town of Philadelphia, Mississippi, prompting a federal investigation of the crimes ("Murder"). Though national media coverage made the public aware of the event leading up to the discovery of the bodies, public remembrance began to fade over time.

Our analysis draws attention to time as a central, constant factor worth noting — the passage of time compounds the public acceptance of narratives that illustrate trauma of the American Black experience. Since public memory can also be understood as "living memory," these memories are "open to contest, revision, and rejection" — a process that often occurs in/through time (Phillips 2). Moreover, these three cases reveal how a countermemory faces greater challenges in becoming accepted as established, collective memory the longer it exists as a countermemory. Finally, their prominence stresses the influence these narratives have on how we view and apply historical context today with regard to public memory. As James Loewen states, "what a community erects on its historical landscape not only sums up its view of the past but also influences its possible futures" (14). Generational narratives are powerful; thus, how we memorialize the present can dramatically impact the way future generations perceive people and events. Without the luxury of consistently and impartially relaying historical information, including Black narratives, we must operate in a non-linear method given the absence of Black perspectives from many historic sources.

For example, Bass Reeves died on January 12, 1910, and only began to officially enter the sphere of public memory over 100 years later when a memorial statue was unveiled on May 26, 2012, in Fort Smith, Arkansas (Whitten). Similarly, The Tulsa Race Massacre took place on May 31 and June 1, 1921, but the foundation of the Tulsa Race Massacre Centennial Commission was formed in 2016, ultimately leading to the construction of Greenwood Rising, a museum commemorating the event, which opened in late 2021 (Krehbiel). In addition to local support from committees and communities, both Reeves and the Tulsa Race Massacre received national attention in public memory through a depiction of the event on HBO's *Watchmen* series in 2019 and a well-regarded Tom Hanks opinion piece in *The New York Times* in June 2021. Similar to the previous examples, the Freedom Summer Murders occurred on June 21, 1964, and despite the lack of support from residents of the town where the murders occurred, *Mississippi Burning,* the feature film based on the events, was released December 9, 1988, six months after the 25th anniversary of the murders. Accordingly, it is important to focus on the role time plays. Which is to say, Black historical events take a long time to reach new light when buried under generational repression. If we accept time as an obstacle for countermemory, the question remains: At what point does a countermemory become part of the larger public memory, and what does it take to make this movement? In addition, how did these narratives come to achieve more exposure, so much so, their memory can no longer be denied in the public sphere? And lastly, what factors should we consider when noting this development?

Categorically, we cannot "rank" the significance of the referenced events. Ranking them is not as significant as registering them. Rather, the point is to account for their resonance as told through regional and national perspectives.

Rhetoric, Media, and Public Memory

For our examination, the fundamental mode through which negotiations occur is in media (film and television in particular) but we also explore two additional factors that shape countermemory acceptance: exposure (the scope and success of narratives, including film adaptations, museums, including the visibility of these depictions) and community engagement (the local, grassroot support of residents in and around areas impacted by the events or individuals). As these examples reveal, countermemories face challenges due to the permanent traces left by traditional historical narratives. Media plays an important part in challenging traditional narratives because it can explore those traces and make them malleable. Moreover, countermemory exposure and community engagement - as parts of the media network, so to speak - further the conversation that allows foundational assumptions to be challenged, discussed, and enhanced.

Undoubtedly, digital forms of public memory have the capacity for more widespread impact (Haskins; Lueck et al.). While Haskins primarily focuses on the ways in which the internet has created digital memory, we would argue that her perspective is also evident in other forms of media, like film and television. Following Haskins' argument, media like *Watchman* and *Mississippi Burning* become a part of public memory, especially when registered alongside more traditional artifacts, like the monument in Fort Smith. In fact, these contemporary forms of public memory have the potential to dramatically impact the way we remember history because we can access these narratives any time and as many times as we want. We do not have to travel to Fort Smith to be educated about Bass Reeves' significance. One caveat, though, is that we must be aware of how many creative liberties a particular media has taken, especially in light of inaccurate representations (see *Braveheart, Last of the Mohicans,* etc.).

Since these media forms are essentially moving images, Barbie Zelizer's scholarship that depicts visual images as having a "voice" is key to our analysis. For Zelizer, this notion of "voice" is how we can understand the role of images in memory; voice is what motivates viewers to link certain images with other events or places. Thus, voice helps viewers recognize the meaning and qualification of an image (162). In Zelizer's application of this principle to images from 9/11, she also argues that certain images stick in our memory because they help us make sense of the horror of that day (178). Applying these ideas to media like *Watchman* or *Mississippi Burning,* we contend that the presence of voice in these media portrayals allow visitors to make contemporary connections to issues of racism that continue to negatively impact our culture. Furthermore, the use of voice in these media portrayals also helps viewers to consider the significance of Black narratives and potentially move them from countermemory to more mainstream perception of public memory. Incorporating events from the past into our cultural memory, as represented in *Watchman* or *Missis-*

sippi Burning, yields a broader historical context that highlights the evolution of our societal growth, particularly for future generations. This trajectory affords our culture the opportunity to understand and compare societal progress, not only based on contemporary standards but the scope of the evolution of our cultural memory.

O'Brien and Sanchez define countermemory as "a marginalized (or often erased) form of remembering…that resituates the narratives of the oppressed or forgotten as equal to dominant narratives… characterized by a challenging—even a disruption—of dominant historical narratives" (5- 8). The rhetoric in this description, "challenging" and "disruption," highlights the work required to influence established narratives and reform public opinion. We could extricate the phrase "dominant narratives" as paramount, and theoretically, a conversion of this systematic ideology could merit a reconsideration of historic events, places, and people. Like the process of relaying historical information itself, public memory dovetails with popular culture, which is interpretive, evolving, and highly influential to current events. Popular culture, as mediated through entertainment, is our dominant narrative. Moreover, it can recklessly reference historic events and individuals for entertainment's sake rather than responsible accuracy. Creative licenses often blemish the validity of public memory and history.

Accordingly, the narratives we use to learn about ourselves can be flawed yet necessary since none of us is without a history and "we're always standing in some place in our lives and there is always a tale of how we came to stand there" (Corder 16). But there is also the responsibility of generational resonance as "virtually all studies of public memory places take account of the connections memory places draw between past and present (Dickinson et al. 30). Place constitutes a significant role in public memory, especially in terms of how narratives are shaped. This places the burden of responsibility on the present generation to reach future generations as much as it does to honor past events and individuals. In short, our public memories are histories, and we must remember how public memory is influenced by shared interpretations and depictions of historical individuals and events. Especially when, nowadays, national television programs gather more viewership through entertainment than local telecasts or newspaper articles containing the same information but remain motivated to inform do. Thus, countermemory faces the same challenges given that our collective understanding of history is muddled by a culture of interpretation as truth (rather than interpretation of truth). In other words, creative license with history is useful but can take us in a useless direction if we don't pause to consider the distinction between interpretation and truth when it comes to our forms of entertainment. It is not necessary for entertainment avenues and public memory interpretations to be exclusive, but there are resonant responsibilities that media should consider when depicting events that have been inadequately presented in public memory throughout the years.

Exposure is central to public memory since the existence of a narrative introduces the idea of a subject, and from there, the idea "lives" within its subjects. In other words, publicity enhances the narrative. Through social progression and successive entertainment outlets, "commercial representations of popular memory have become increasingly diversified and now speak directly to social groups that have been historically marginalized in the broader cultural currents of mainstream society" (Thompson and Tian 596). As a result, previously marginalized narratives in popular memory have the ability to reach national audiences. Whereas this progression bodes well for social advancement and acceptance, the celebration of previously erased Black narratives remains an uphill climb if one concedes that our current cultural moment is only beginning to accept these accounts in public memory. Rather, the scope of public memory expands and contracts with the will of society ensuring that the process of entering public memory, let alone changing perceptions of history taught in classrooms, can take years if not lifetimes to impact society. However, accepting and embracing countermemory narratives that comprise a space in public memory offer opportunities to further develop and integrate accounts of historic people and events.

Media Representations

Bass Reeves experienced a surge in popularity that began with a monument unveiling in 2012. In 2019, the film *Hell on the Border* was released (using characters based on Reeves' life) and, in 2019, his character was used by name in Netflix's 2021 *The Harder They Fall* (which opens with this statement: "While the events of this story are fictional... These. People. Existed."). *The Harder They Fall* did little to showcase Reeves' actual accomplishments but did provide name recognition and, upon release, reached 2.5 million U.S. households its first five days of streaming on Netflix (@Samba TV). Furthermore, Reeves was included in the national limelight with his inclusion in the 2019 HBO series *Watchmen* — primarily through a recreated scene from the 1921 silent film *Trust in the Law!* (This scene was playing in a theater and dramatizes Reeves' life, most significantly by way of his arresting a corrupt sheriff onscreen). With tragic coincidence, a literal explosion from the Tulsa Race Massacre interrupts Reeves' scene and the sound of sirens and more explosions appear. This violence foreshadows the horror of the murders of the massacre for the first time reenacted on screen as Black citizens fight for their lives, flee the violence, and ultimately react to the horrors. Finally, with a reported 1.6 million views on the night of the release, *Watchmen* opened the floodgates to more national exposure of the Tulsa Race Massacre through the HBO series *Lovecraft Country,* where characters travel back in time and experience the horrors of the massacre firsthand as their family tries to survive the brutality (Maas). A slew of documentaries were also released in 2021 to commemorate the 100-year anniversary of the tragedy (including The History Channel's *Tulsa Burning: The 1921 Race Massacre* and CNN's *Dreamland: The Burning of Black Wall Street*). Through these visualizations, The Tulsa Race Massacre was depicted in an unprecedented manner. And through these unflinching portrayals of the carnage in full display, The Tulsa Race Massacre of 1921 entered into public memory.

In the case of "The Freedom Summer Murders," the nation was strongly influenced to remember the violent event via a film. The 1988 Hollywood film *Mississippi Burning* "did more than reinvigorate national awareness of the 1964 murders; it renewed national interest in the case, which ultimately placed pressure on the local community to acknowledge the murders" (Whitlinger 655). Additionally, despite critical acclaim and Academy Award nominations, the film remains "arguably better known for having sparked a national debate on the responsibility of filmmakers to accurately portray historical events" (654-655). In a 2021 *New York Times* opinion piece, Academy Award Winner Tom Hanks wrote about the Tulsa Race Massacre and the social significance of responsibly approaching history through Hollywood films. He observed that "historically based fiction entertainment must portray the burden of racism in our nation for the sake of the art form's claims to verisimilitude and authenticity... America's history is messy but knowing that makes us wiser and stronger people." If by societal standards, memories have "arrived" in popular memory following on-screen depictions, then Reeves has not officially been introduced through the medium since awareness of his role in history is just beginning in media contexts. Whereas depictions of both the Freedom Summer Murders and the Tulsa Race Massacre feature the depiction of secular events, it proves to be much more difficult to encapsulate an individual's life story.

In film, the process of telling an individual's story can serve a broader cultural metaphor through the lens of an individual's life story. Biopics, or biographical film portrayals, seek to do just that, and have been a staple in American entertainment culture helping us to better understand broader societal issues and circumstances throughout history. The emotional resonance following the main character in their environment serves as the fuel of the genre, as context and circumstance is at the forefront of the narrative. Celebrated and acclaimed films such as *Schindler's List (1993)*, *Milk (2008)*, and *The Elephant Man (1980)*, have focused on perpetuating the narrative of secular lives under adverse societal conditions through the perspective amidst genocide, homophobia, and alienation, respectively. Similarly, Black historical narratives have been furthered through this style of filmmaking, ushering critical acclaim and cultural resonance including *Malcolm X (1992)*, *Ray (2004)*, *12 Years a Slave (2013)*, and *BlacKkKlansman (2018)*. A biopic of Reeves' life would contribute to the presence of Black narrative in film but also serve to illuminate a period of time, the "Wild West," which is ripe with societal misrepresentations and misconceptions in our public memory.

There have been promising developments to continue evolving the narrative of Bass Reeves., In September 2021, it was announced that award-winning actor David Oyelowo had signed on to play Reeves in a limited series for ViacomCBS and MTV Entertainment Studios (Petski). Reeves, having worked with Indigenous people in his time while pursuing and ultimately arresting outlaws in Apache, Arapaho, Comanche, Kiowa, Osage and Wichita territory represents a departure from conventional "Wild West" storylines depicted in film and media adaptations (McKay). His story personifies a congruence of Black narratives, having escaped from slavery to Native American territory and learning to speak the languages of Indigenous tribes (Burton 6). This ongoing relationship with Native Americans would serve him well, as later, it was necessary to work with Indigenous locals, as "tribal courts had no jurisdiction" over criminals in the territory (xiii). Considering the overlapping narratives of Reeves' history, one could see this culmination of perspectives unfold as building blocks of previous narratives build momentum for a historical narrative which dispels stereotypes. Subsequently, each corresponding depiction carries with it the weight of momentum but also the foundation of support from depictions that predated that particular installment. The acceptance and embrace of previously marginalized Black narratives in film and popular memory creates opportunities to add to the sum of individual and collective perspectives.

Community-Engaged Memory Work

Along with the Bass Reeves memorial in Fort Smith, another statue commemorating Reeves has been underway for three years in Muskogee, Oklahoma, where the statue will be prominently featured on the grounds of Three Rivers Museum. According to Angie Rush, director of Three Rivers Museum, Reeves' legacy is growing, and his resonance with Muskogee residents is strong. "During the time period of Bass' life, slavery and segregation were huge factors. That in itself marginalized his and other African Americans' presence. Our hope for the Statue is that it will bring more awareness not only to Bass Reeves but to all other law enforcement officers thus fostering more conversations." As Lueck et al. argue, place- and community-engaged public memory projects center stakeholders' perspectives about public remembrance and historical representation, so rather than relying solely on media representations of Bass Reeves, Muskogee residents determined for themselves how Reeves will be commemorated (15).

For our purposes, community-engaged memory work refers to the humble, homegrown beginnings of memorials to historic figures and events wherein community members serve as grassroots ambassadors or caretakers. It is not always the case that the memory of these events and individuals rise to prominence given the spirit of domestic unity. As Lueck et al. remind us, "community-engaged memory work is complicated, fraught with potential power differentials and needful of a careful personal and political approach" (15). The divisions that arise in public narratives, especially when proximity and pride are associated, complicate the control and ownership of these memories. This process is further complicated when communities' established narrative remains separated after a memorial is established (and the chasm between public memory and countermemory is further deepened). In many cases, the chasm is the result of white people in positions of power who do not support the truth-telling efforts of countermemory. But, as Michelle Angela Oriz reminds us: "Stories are powerful, especially within the context that they are told or represented" (37). The origin of this tension, regardless of timing in relation to the opening of the memorial, is inconsequential since the "disruption" has already occurred. Ensuing emotional responses, either in favor of or opposition to the memorial, opens the door to both conversation and contestation. Conversations between members of the community can be malleable and illuminating, creating new opportunities for perspective and growth, whereas contestation can quickly become muddled, introducing combustible emotional outbursts, forcing opponents to dig in their heels at change, resulting in stunted societal growth. Ultimately, this boils down to marginalized narratives being represented and celebrated on a civic level as opposed to keeping things as they were, without the embrace of these narratives. From the cases identified, both sides of the reaction were examined, as will be further explored.

The community of Fort Smith, Arkansas organized "The Bass Reeves Legacy Initiative" in 2010. According to Internet archives, this Public Benefit Corporation registered with the State of Arkansas to raise money for a memorial to Reeves as a local hero. Local business owners, elected officials, and interested community individuals formed the committee which set their sights on funding the Bass Reeves memorial statue, which totaled $300,000 (Whitten). Through years of work, and with assistance from civic leaders for subsidiary costs (such as the plaque and statue base), the committee secured funding through private donations raised through various community events. At the memorial unveiling on May 26, 2012, the weight of community expectations and efforts fell in unison with the shroud which covered the statue – committee members were rewarded by a local hero recreated in bronze and undeniably etched into history (Holmes). At the memorial unveiling, Reeves historian and author Art Burton said, "The more he's embraced by the local community... that helps establish who Bass Reeves is, and I do believe that's going to blossom and we'll get more of a national perspective on Bass" (Holmes). Whereas the memorial was a considerable undertaking for committee members, supporters, like Burton, understand the significance of the statue's existence as proof of Reeves' entrance and ascent into public memory.

The community spirit was strong in Tulsa, Oklahoma when, according to the organization's website, the 1921 Tulsa Race Massacre Centennial Commission was founded in 2016 under the leadership of Senator Kevin Matthews. Through community and corporate donations, the Centennial Commission raised $30 million, with $18.2 million spent on the new history center, Greenwood Rising--the flagship project of the Centennial Commission. The freestanding facility sits on land donated by The Hille Foundation, a private, family foundation organization dedicated to supporting non-profit organizations and projects in the Tulsa area (Hille Foundation). Greenwood Rising is considered a world-class history center that serves as gateway to Tulsa's Historic Greenwood District. According to the organization's website, the facility "honors the icons of Black Wall Street, memorializes the victims of the massacre, and examines the lessons of the past to inspire meaningful, sustainable action in the present." According to the Greenwood Rising website, the Centennial Commission ceased operations on June 30, 2021, making way for a 501(c)3 nonprofit organization to continue the legacy of the public memory of the massacre. As with the Bass Reeves monument, this structure serves as a home for the memory of the victims and a tangible reminder of past events. Recently, Greenwood Rising finished seventh in a nationwide vote for USA Today's "Best New Attraction of 2021" marking a bold entrance into public memory. Categorizing the museum as an "attraction" offers pause to remember the blurred distinction between history and entertainment. The fusion of genres is indicative of the power and reach of the message.

The Black community of Philadelphia, Mississippi commemorated "The Freedom Summer Murders" through an annual event which, since 1964, is a considerable labor of love for many (Whitlinger 649). However, this event was not always embraced by the community at large. The film *Mississippi Burning* generated national interest which forced the hands of residents to accept the reality of the event rather than keep it buried in the past. This response speaks to the power of collective public memory as many "closest" to the scene of the crime could not be mindfully more far away from public memory. Before the film's release, the town "could be described as having two mnemonic communities: the African-American community, which commemorated the event annually, and the white community, which remained shrouded in civic silence" (Whitlinger 653). The national spotlight drew attention to this small town of 7,000 residents and on June 21, 1989, over 1,000 people nationwide descended to participate in the first citywide commemoration service marking the twenty-fifth anniversary of the murders (659). The film exposed the events of this town to a national audience and, as a result, prompted a response that created an organized approach that was lacking at the local level before the film's release.

The juxtaposition between community-engaged memory work and retrospective memory work (spawned from the release of *Mississippi Burning*) highlight the uniqueness of circumstance surrounding a historic person or act. Where these memory works dovetail is the resonance on our collective cultural memory. There is no doubt a blockbuster film will initially reach a broader audience than a local museum or memorial, but it is necessary to localize the subject of the film and create a "home" for the historic person or act. On a broader scale, as necessary as it is to introduce an audience to a marginalized historic person or act, it is just as important to properly localize the subject, which can often be more challenging. In the example of Greenwood Rising, despite the level of success and recognition the facility has garnered, not all Tulsa residents approve of the way the facility is marketed and operating. According to a recent article, survivors and descendants of victims of the Tulsa Race Massacre sued the city of Tulsa and other individuals, seeking "acknowledgment that the defendants' policies, actions, and inactions deprived them of wealth and created inequitable health, education, housing, and employment conditions that can and should be remedied today" (Human). Furthermore, the survivors and descendants seek ". . . restitution for the harm caused and lives and property lost, as well as an injunction preventing the defendants from exploiting the likeness of victims and legacy of the massacre for economic gain, particularly to raise funds for Greenwood Rising" (Human Rights Watch). These developments highlight the importance and complications of adequately obtaining a variety of community dedication and involvement to further the cause of the memorial.

Applications

When studying the narratives evident in The Freedom Summer Murders, The Tulsa Race Massacre, and the life story of Bass Reeves, significant correlations emerge. The way these historic events, places, and people ultimately became incorporated into public memory speaks to a culmination of progressive advancements through time, exposure, and community engagement. As such, each subsequent act effectively expanded the scope of public memory, though the process was neither steadfast nor linear. The lack of community engagement as well as the relatively short passage of time between historic events and film adaptation make The Freedom Summer Murders an outlier. The occurrence of the murders in relation to the release of the film based on the events, June 21, 1964, and December 9, 1988, respectively, was a comparatively short amount of time. Additionally, the film thrust awareness of The Freedom Summer Murders into the national spotlight without the support of the local community; the film served as both an introduction and a catalyst for further challenging conversations. The Tulsa Race Massacre and the life story of Bass Reeves were first championed locally as these Black narratives grew organically from their respective communities. From this growth, national recognition then followed, with nearly 100 years between these historic events occurring prior to being integrated into public memory through national television programs. Ultimately, one could argue Bass Reeves has not yet breached public memory, but indications are positive.

What seems uncontested is the reach of visual entertainment avenues, both the silver screen in 1988 through the release of *Mississippi Burning* and the small screen's run of HBO's *Watchmen* in 2019 were agents for influencing and shaping public memory of Black narratives to national audiences. In the 31 years between the theatrical release of *Mississippi Burning* and the television debut of *Watchmen,* many cultural and societal advancements have occurred, in addition to communication applications such as social media, but the resonance of visual mediums hold a dominant cultural influence. Whereas proximity or the localness of community engagement may no longer be necessary for gaining support of Black narratives as a result of tools such as social media and online communications, technology alone was not enough to impact public memory of The Tulsa Race Massacre prior to *Watchmen* and it still hasn't provided enough influence to make Bass Reeves a household name regardless of the wealth of information available. Perhaps it is less about the information contained in the message but rather the method of delivery via a visual platform, as it is one thing to ask an audience to read about a distressing series of racially motivated murders but another experience when these events play out organically on screens in living rooms, kitchens, and bedrooms across the world. The unflinching brutality proved to be undeniable. Additional Black narratives should expect equal resonance through visual depictions in similar formats, and in Reeves' case, the light of his heroism in spite of the darkness of both racial prejudice and everyday ruthlessness of the time would be a worthy juxtaposition. It is also crucial to note depictions in *Mississippi Burning* and *Watchmen* did not oversell or enhance these historic events, but simply acted to demonstrate visual depictions of the events. In fairness, *Mississippi Burning* is not a verbatim depiction of events of The Freedom Summer Murders, but this is not vital; the byproduct of the film and its related sentiments opened access to public memory. Others have followed, and through this formula, many more events could garner similar impacts on public memory.

Conclusion

Collectively, the public memory of Bass Reeves, the Tulsa Race Massacre, and the Freedom Summer Murders have entered various stages of public memory. They serve as examples of how patterns emerge and can inform us as to how future countermemories might be received. Though we can't discount the course of progress resulting from continued exposure and levels of community engagement, the momentum these events and individuals received has impacted the sphere of public memory. Whereas media and film depictions furthered the narrative of the Tulsa Race Massacre and the Freedom Summer Murders, Bass Reeves has not broken through public memory as a household name, though this could change following the debut of Reeves' streaming programs, as enthusiasm for his memory is on the side of progress. As mentioned, Hollywood depictions can force an agenda as well as corroborate a grassroots initiative. Moreover, community engagement and exposure act as catalysts for one another but can, less effectively, develop on their own, separate terms. Ultimately, previously marginalized Black narratives are enjoying unmatched support in public memory and these developments will shape how future generations view history moving forward. But complacency will halt progress and supporters of countermemory must gain momentum to push more countermemories into the realm of public memory. Vigilance is key because there are many more stories to tell of those whose histories are excluded. And yet, these histories have a place in what we call the public and what we collectively determine and negotiate public memory—that continually evolving construct—to be.

Works Cited

"Best New Attraction of 2021? SkyFly: Soar America": ." *USA TODAY: 10BEST*, 31 Dec. 2021, https://www.10best.com/awards/travel/best-new-attraction/. Accessed 7 Sept. 2024.

Burton, Art. *Black Gun, Silver Star: The Life and Legend of Frontier Marshal Bass Reeves*. University of Nebraska Press, 2006.

Corder, James W. "Argument as Emergence, Rhetoric as Love." *Rhetoric Review*, vol. 4, no. 1, 1985, pp. 16–32.

Dickinson, Greg, et al. *Places of Public Memory: The Rhetoric of Museums and Memorials*. University of Alabama Press. 2010.

Dickenson, Greg, et al.. "Spaces of Remembering and Forgetting: The Reverent Eye/I at the Plains Indian Museum." *Communication and Critical/Cultural Studies*, vol 3, no. 1, year, pp. 227-47.

Edbauer, Jenny. "Unframing Models of Public Distribution: From Rhetorical Situation to Rhetorical Ecologies." *Rhetoric Society Quarterly*, vol 35, no. 4, year, pp. 5-24.

Gruenewald, Tim. *Curating America's Painful Past: Memory, Museums, and the National Imagination*. Lawrence, University Press of Kansas, 2021.

Hanks, Tom. "You Should Learn the Truth About the Tulsa Race Massacre." *The New York Times*, 4 June 2021, https://www.nytimes.com/2021/06/04/opinion/

tom-hanks-tulsa-race-massacre-history.html?searchResultPosition=7. Accessed March 12, 2022.

Haskins, Ekaterina. "Between Archives and Participation: Public Memory in a Digital Age." *Rhetoric Society Quarterly,* vol. 37, no. 4, 2007, year, pp. 401-422.

Human Rights Watch. "US: Failed Justice 100 Years After Tulsa Race Massacre." *Human Rights Watch,* 21 May 2021, https://www.hrw.org/news/2021/05/21/us-failed-justice-100-years-after-tulsa-race-massacre. Accessed 22 Jan 2024.

Krehbiel, Randy. "Watch Now: Greenwood Rising Makes 'Spellbinding' Formal Opening." *Tulsa World,* Tulsa World, 9 Sept. 2022, https://tulsaworld.com/news/local/racemassacre/watch-now-greenwood-rising-makes-spellbinding-formal-opening/article_000be0d4-f467-11eb-923e-9f83291a6f12.html. Accessed 7 Sept. 2024.

Loewen, James W. *Lies Across America: What Our Historic Sites and National Monuments Get Wrong.* New York, Touchstone. 1999.

Lueck, Amy, et al. "Public Memory as Community-Engaged Writing: Composing Difficult Histories on Campus." *Community Literacy Journal,* vol. 15, no. 2, 2021, pp. 9-30.

Maas, Jennifer. "'Watchmen' Finale Tops Series Premiere with 1.6 Million Multiplatform Viewers." *TheWrap,* The Wrap News Inc., 16 Dec. 2019, https://www.thewrap.com/watchmen-season-1-finale-ratings-viewers-hbo/. Accessed 7 Sept. 2024.

McKay, Dwanna L. "Oklahoma Is – and Always Has Been – Native Land." *The Conversation,* The Conversation, 13 Sept. 2022, https://theconversation.com/oklahoma-is-and-always-has-been-native-land-142546.

O'Brien, April L. "Exclusionary Public Memory Documents: Orientating Historical Marker Texts Within a Technical Communication Framework." *Technical Communication Quarterly,* vol. 31, no. 2, 2021, pp. 111–125.

O'Brien, April and James Chase Sanchez. "Racial Countermemory: Tourism, Spatial Design, and Hegemonic Remembering." *Journal of Multimodal Rhetorics,* vol. 5, no. 2, 2022, http://journalofmultimodalrhetorics.com/5-2-issue-o-brien-and-sanchez. Accessed 7 Sept. 2024.

Oriz, Michelle Angela. "Amplifying Community Voices Through Public Art." *Community Literacy Journal,* vol. 14, no. 2, 2020, pp. 25-37.

Petski, Denise. "David Oyelowo to Star in 'Bass Reeves' Limited Series from Taylor Sheridan as Part of Yoruba Saxon Overall Deal with ViacomCBS & MTV Entertainment Studios." *Deadline,* Deadline, 9 Sept. 2021, https://deadline.com/2021/09/david-oyelowo-star-bass-reeves-limited-series-taylor-sheridan-overall-deal-viacomcbs-mtv-entertainment-studios-1234829404/. Accessed 7 Sept. 2024.

Phillips, Kendall, editor. *Framing Public Memory.* Tuscaloosa, University of Alabama Press, 2004.

Poirot, Kristan and Shevaun Watson. "Memories of Freedom and White Resilience: Place, Tourism, and Urban Slavery." *Rhetoric Society Quarterly,* vol. 45, no. 2, 2015, pp. 91-116.

Rush, Angie. Bass Reeves Memorial. xx Jan. xxxx. Telephone Interview.

@Samba TV (Sohaib Athar). "2.5M US households watched #TheHarderTheyFall in its first 5 days streaming on Netflix. The film's viewership skewed female (+8%), and households with Black viewers over-indexed by +111%." *Twitter,* 8 Nov. 2021, 3:13pm. p.m. twitter.com/reallyvirtual/status/64780730286358528?lang=en.

Tell, Dave. *Remembering Emmett Till.* Chicago, University of Chicago Press, 2019.

Thompson, Craig & Kelly Tian. "Reconstructing the South: How Commercial Myths Compete for Identity Value Through the Ideological Shaping of Popular Memories and Countermemories." *Journal of Consumer Research,* vol. 34,n. 5, 2008, pp. 595–613.

"Tulsa's Historic Greenwood District." *Oklahoma Black History,* Oklahoma Black History Resource, https://oklahomablackhistory.org/tulsa-greenwood-district/. Accessed 7 Sept. 2024.

Whitlinger, Claire. "From Countermemory to Collective Memory: Acknowledging the 'Mississippi Burning' Murders." *Sociological Forum,* vol. 30, no. S1, 2015, pp. 648–670.

—. "The Transformative Capacity of Commemoration: Comparing Mnemonic Activism in Philadelphia, Mississippi." *Mobilization: An International Quarterly,* vol. 24, no. 4, 2019, pp. 455–474.

Whitten, Christine. "Bass Reeves Legacy Monument Unveiled." *5newsonline.com,* KFSM-TV, 26 May 2012, https://www.5newsonline.com/article/news/local/outreach/back-to-school/bass-reeves-legacy-monument-revealed/527-3bfa649d-9c31-4fd1-80f0-85dddfbe9797. Accessed 7 Sept. 2024.

Zelizer, Barbue. "The Voice of the Visual in Memory." *Framing Public Memory,* edited by Kendell Phillips, University of Alabama Press, 2004, pp. 157-186.

Author Bios

Elliott Cochran is a nomadic communications professional in southeast Texas. Relying on the strength of his interpersonal skills, he held positions in daily newspapers, public relations, and higher education. He received his Bachelor of Arts in Journalism from Texas Tech University in 2008 and his Master of Arts in Technical Communication from Sam Houston State University in 2023. His graduate work examined adaptability and audience awareness as a gateway to empathy, yielding a better understanding of the applicability and importance of empathy in technical communication. He continues to apply his studies as an instructional designer at SHSU Online.

April L. O'Brien is an assistant professor at Sam Houston State University. Her research and teaching interests include public memory, countermemory, technical and professional communication, and social justice. She has published in *Technical Communication Quarterly, Technical Communication & Social Justice, Technical Communication, enculturation,* and others. Her current co-authored book project theorizes a rhetoric of countermemory.

"To Open Eyes": Community Literacies, Radical Democracy, and a Pedagogy Presence at Black Mountain College, 1933–1957

Angela Muir

Abstract

This article examines the transformative educational practices and democratic ethos of Black Mountain College, an experimental institution ahead of its time. Drawing on insights from scholars like Rhea Estelle Lathan and Susan Kates, Muir positions Black Mountain as a site of community literacies, by prioritizing democratic engagement, diversity, and experiential learning. The article explores how Black Mountain, amidst the socio-political tumult of the mid-20th century, fostered a dynamic environment centered on art, community, and individualized learning. By unpacking Black Mountain's foundational values and meticulous analysis of archival materials and educational theories, Muir highlights the pedagogical innovations of figures like Josef Albers, whose "Pedagogy of Presence" emphasized perception, process, and abstraction, nurturing not only artistic expression but also critical citizenship. Muir invites readers to reconsider the role of education in fostering democracy, inclusivity, and social change.

Keywords: community literacies, service, collaboration, democracy, citizenship, contemplative, pedagogy, social change, Black Mountain College

> *I concede that several contemporary literacy scholars have begun broadening the domain in which literacy is situated. These studies suggest there is a great deal of complex literacy activity occurring outside standard academic contexts, as well as what constitutes "community literacy" within local communities. However, standard frameworks traditionally follow a "master framework," marginalizing or ignoring "other" ways of knowing.*
>
> —Rhea Estelle Lathan, "Testimony as a Sponsor of Literacy"

> *If we must accept education as life and as preparation for life, we must relate all school work, including work in art, as closely as possible to modern problems.*
>
> —Josef Albers, "Teaching Form Through Practice"

Consider the possibility that in 1933, there was an academic institution centered around art, community building, individually tailored curriculums, and democracy. Now imagine that this place was also a refuge for immigrants and was racially integrated in 1944, a decade before Brown v. Board of Education. Black Mountain College, an experimental liberal arts college in the Black Mountain foothills of North Carolina, was such a place.

I begin this article with epigraphs from Rhea Estelle Lathan and Josef Albers because at the intersection of what they say is the goal of this essay: to make a case for Black Mountain College as a community literacy site by the model of its principles and emergent pedagogy. Within the field of composition and rhetoric, many scholars are working to expand the definition of literacy and provide examples of useful frames for consideration and study. Among them, Lathan, as well as Susan Kates, Stephen Schneider, and Candace Epps-Robertson, explore the literacy schools of the Civil Rights Movement to exemplify the connection between literacy and activism. Epps-Robertson establishes that critical pedagogies can challenge power dynamics by giving students access to skills that will prepare them for life. She concludes, "[p]edagogical and curricula recovery work is important because of its ability to help us recover voices, sites, and movements that have traditionally been marginalized or shadowed by dominant histories"(91). Jessica Pauszek forwards this sentiment and, through her exploration of Pecket Well College, adds the angle of working-class literacy and the principles of "collective organizing, peer learning, and a belief in equal participation" (657). These examples lead us to consider the role of education in democracy: the development of community members and active citizens empowered to make decisions and solve problems.

While the Prince Edward County Free School, Highlander Folk School, Sea Island Citizenship School, and Pecket Well College have been presented in scholarship as community literacy sites, I believe Black Mountain College is another example worth exploring. Though not technically centered around reading and writing literacy, Black Mountain aimed to create core organizational literacies that placed democracy at the center and resituated hierarchies to centralize learning over power. Not only did it obtain diversity standards unheard of for its time, but it also practiced an open curriculum long before the conversation gained traction. Black Mountain shows us that service and collaboration within academia's walls are crucial to building a productive democratic community. Finally, and most importantly, it provides an example of a contemplative pedagogy, which "place[s] the student in the center of his or her learning so that the student can connect his or her inner world to the outer world" (Barbezat and Bush, 6), that supported the development of craft and community citizenship.

The pedagogical literacies offered at Black Mountain were designed for holistic education. Albers, an art educator and pedagogical theorist, worked at Black Mountain to establish what I call a *Pedagogy of Presence*, which attempted to solve "modern problems" by studying perception, process, and abstraction. The crux of this pedagogy demands a presence from both student and instructor, an early example of contemplative practice in higher education. The result of this approach to learning was not only to "open eyes," as Albers says, but also a mastery of form and a product that responded to "modern problems," which resulted in antiracist literacies and activism in action.

Black Mountain endured throughout a period wrought with national and international tension. After its closure in 1957, the United States underwent a dynamic time of change, and perhaps we can see our current predicament in similar terms. This essay places Black Mountain as a model site for community literacy because it provides literacies central to creating community in higher education. I overview the organizational literacies through the school's origins and structural values, describe the service and collaboration literacies, and highlight a specific pedagogical literacy that emerged from the democratic framework. Finally, I reflect on how these explored values and pedagogy resulted in antiracist literacies and activism, which should be relevant to composition and rhetoric scholars, as well as education theorists and social historians, as a site for further exploration.

Organizational Literacies: "Radical Democracy in Action"

Since the turn toward democracy in rhetoric and composition studies, scholars such as Rachel Reidner, Kevin Mahoney, and Susan Wells have pointed us to Freire, Gramsci, and Derrida to suggest that "*Democracies to Come* emerge between the fields of cultural studies and rhetoric and composition" (9). Black Mountain is a perfect example of this, where historical context, values, and pedagogy intersect to produce a model where we see "learning as a practice of and for freedom" (9) that "creates ways of knowing that suggest political possibilities" (3). Radical democracy at Black Mountain was enacted first in the framework and guiding principles.

In 1933, the United States was amidst the worst year of the Great Depression, the Third Reich had come into power in Germany, and John Andrew Rice founded Black Mountain College in North Carolina. Rice had been recently dismissed from Rollins College for refusing to sign a loyalty pledge that he felt was not in the best interest of his students. Rice had a relatively progressive and controversial view of academic measures; he considered "regulations the last refuge of mediocrity," he disdained "numerologists in education," and thought that learning should happen "in one's own way and according to one's own timetable" (Duberman 5). His aim at educating students had more to do with forming their emotional intelligence and problem-solving skills than mastering subject knowledge. After months of toying with the nagging sentiment that he should put his theories into action, he finally approached his encouraging colleagues with the idea of opening Black Mountain. After months of work, the lease was signed on August 24, 1933, and Black Mountain College was officially founded.

From the perspectives of fellow academic administrations and the surrounding community, Black Mountain's enrollment and hiring policies were considered controversial. It sought to enroll and hire both men and women and offered refuge to Jewish immigrants fleeing Nazi Germany, becoming a haven for cultural differences. Black Mountain admitted the first Black student in 1944 and employed many Black instructors as early as 1945. For the Jim Crow South, these were landmark events that did not come without pushback, such as threats of violence and protest. Nevertheless, the founding ideologies and actions set the precedent that the board, which was made up of both students and instructors, was to follow democratic practices in decision-making and social responsibility.

Black Mountain's interdisciplinary approach enabled students to direct their own learning. Without a core set of requirements, referred to as an open curriculum, students were made active in their education. It was a democratic system where students were empowered to direct their learning. Will Hamlin, a Black Mountain student, said of this methodology, "Academically, I don't think we suffered from having the freedom to study whatever we wanted to study… There was a sense of involvement in Black Mountain classes. You were there because this was something you were interested in" (Duberman 100). Freedom of choice sets up a model that mirrors life, requiring discernment and confidence. In addition, it establishes a system of trust between the student and the institution and encourages collaboration to reach learning goals. In short, asking students to explore their interests and priorities, exercise good decision-making skills, and take ownership of experiences and community participation prepares them for citizenship outside academic walls.

Black Mountain aimed to dismantle hierarchies and encourage democracy in every aspect of its structure. Students and instructors held equal positions on the board, worked side by side on building and farming, sat together in the cafeteria, and cooperated on creative projects. This effectively endorsed a sense of freedom and a blending of the public/private and personal/political. This was, at times, chaotic and not always harmonious. Still, it positions the college as "a living example of radical democracy in action, an experiment in the practice of community that requires neither consensus nor harmony" (Molesworth 49).

Furthermore, the policies and values for the students were the same policies and values for the teachers. Many instructors took classes in other disciplines while they taught at the college. Notable examples are English literature lecturer M.C. Richards, who studied pottery at Black Mountain with Karen Karnes and David Weinrib, and writer Charles Olson who studied dance with Merce Cunningham. Instructors taking courses alongside students established a mutual respect for both study and instruction while encouraging collaboration.

Collaboration & Service Literacies: Happenings

Black Mountain's central organizational aim was to provide a "holistic" model, educating the "whole person" by encouraging service and collaboration. At Black Mountain, holistic education blended curriculum and extracurriculars. By keeping the students engaged outside of the classroom in duties around the community, the students were not only gaining skills but were also learning to see their impact on the larger group. In Susan Kates's article "Literacy, Voting Rights, and the Citizenship Schools in the South, 1957–1970," she posits that "service learning" and "service-oriented endeavors" call for "reciprocity and community empowerment," which is essential in education (499). Similarly, John Dewey writes,

> unless [the] end is placed in the context of service rendered to others, skills gained will be put to an egoistic and selfish use and may be employed as means of a trained shrewdness in which one person gets the better of others. Too often, indeed, the schools, through reliance upon the spur of competition and bestowing special honors and prizes, only build up and strengthen the disposition that makes an individual, when he leaves school, employ his special talents and superior skill to outwit his fellows without respect for the welfare of others (11).

At Black Mountain, students worked with faculty to build the structures that became classrooms and housing. They planted and harvested the food they would eventually use in the kitchen. They shared the responsibility of cooking and serving meals or cleaning the mess hall alongside the faculty. Everyone was involved in the running of the community, centralizing a service mindset.

Drawing from the insights of Kates and Dewey, service to others, in the context of art, shifts away from the traditional definition of art as "self-expression," and instead, expression becomes a byproduct of the experience. A famous example of this is the "happenings" at Black Mountain, a free-to-all performance in service of the community.

The "happenings" embodied the essence of Black Mountain: art centrality, an interdisciplinary experience, free community entertainment, and a non-hierarchical cast of talent. Teachers and students would perform alongside one another without distinction. The "happenings" were based on the doctrine that "art is completed by the observer" (Duberman 370) and developed in a conversation between composer John Cage and pianist David Tudor. Cage would outline the "happening" into time brackets and then invite various artists to fill the time, all acting "by means of chance operations" (Duberman 370). For example, one famous performance included readings by Charles Olson and M.C. Richards, paintings by Robert Rauschenberg, piano compositions by Cage and Tudor, and a dance number by Merce Cunningham. Cage's aim was "purposeless purposefulness." Performances were not recorded, and recollections of these experiences varied wildly. Each artist and audience member would recall different details, demonstrating diverse perceptions and focus. Not recording was also an act of resistance to history, a way to disentangle power and hierarchy.

With art education at the core, Black Mountain modeled how creativity could be experienced, not as isolated instances, but as central to all life. The 1933 Black Mountain Catalogue speaks to the central role creativity can play in life through the following statement:

> Dramatics, Music, and the Fine Arts, which often exist precariously on the fringes of the curriculum, are regarded as an integral part of the life of the College...through some kind of art experience... the student can come to the realization of order in the world; and, by being sensitized to movement,

form, sound, and the other media of the arts, gets a firmer control of himself and his environment than is possible through purely intellectual effort.

All students, whether they considered themselves artists or economists, would actively experience the arts. This points to a measure of student potential not as an endpoint but as an integrated process or method. It also foregrounded a pedagogical framework that championed new ways of seeing and being in the world.

Pedagogical Literacies: Pedagogy of Presence

Composition studies have engaged contemplative pedagogies since before they were labeled as such in the forms of freewriting and introspection. Scholars such as Robert Yagelski and Paula Mathieu have helped shape how we see these pedagogies function inside the classroom. When integrating contemplative practices, Mathieu explains that by "developing compassion and exploring empathy," we shift to awareness. She goes on to illuminate that this is a move away from "thinking" and toward *presence*. She says of mindful practices, "thinking and the intellect are the very problem they seek to counter. They are fundamentally about what could be called *awareness*. About being fully present—as a writer or a teacher—in the current moment, and not preoccupied with thoughts of the past or future" ("Being There," 15).

With this consideration as my guide, I see a contemplative pedagogy that emerged from within Black Mountain College's core values. I have termed it the *Pedagogy of Presence* because it requires teachers and students to rely on a fully immersive learning experience or *awareness*. Perception, process, and abstraction are the three pillars of this pedagogy, and one can see how these three elements function by examining the methods used at Black Mountain College. These organizational values of Black Mountain set the stage for the *Pedagogy of Presence* to materialize. This pedagogy can be best outlined through the methods used by Josef Albers. Though Albers worked with fine art rather than writing, his practices could easily be applied to composition studies or almost any other discipline. For this reason, I believe it demands our close attention. Albers's pedagogy was a method of instructing art while educating the whole person through offering an experiential course for learning to see (perception), working with a medium (process), and creating a product (abstraction).

Josef Albers, an already distinguished art teacher at the Bauhaus in Germany, was asked by John Rice to teach at Black Mountain via telegram in 1933. Albers had recently lost his position at the Bauhaus as it had closed to avoid accepting Nazi instructors. Albers and his wife Anni were consequently looking for a reason to leave Germany to avoid conflict over Anni's Jewish heritage. Josef spoke little English, but when he arrived in North Carolina fresh from Berlin, he told newspapers, "I want to open eyes." This simple statement was the core trait of his approach to instruction. He believed that "academic studies under academic teachers, and academic methods, and for academic measurements will produce school stars which will wane after school. Any work done for the sake of the teacher, or the sake of the school is not enduring, because life is everything but academic" (Albers, *Abstract Art*). For Albers, a community setting such as Black Mountain was an ideal place to enact his philosophy.

Albers held that self-expression should not be taught as central to the arts; instead, an understanding of direct observation and self-discovery were vital. Art is not simply a result of imitation or reproduction but a communication of feeling. This enactment would find the best results in training the eyes and the hands. He says, "art is a province in which one finds all the problems of life reflected—not only the problems of form (e.g., proportion and balance) but also spiritual problems (e.g. of philosophy, of religion, of sociology, of economy)" (*Concerning Art Instruction*). This makes art a rich medium for general education and development and a pillar for community literacy.

Josef Albers's "open eyes" pedagogy was made clear in the 1934 Black Mountain Bulletin, "Concerning Art Instruction." Albers writes, "our art instruction attempts first to teach the student to see in the widest sense: to open his eyes to the phenomena about him and, most important of all, to open to his own living, being and doing." Therefore, experimenting with the "branches of art" and confronting fundamental problems gives students a window into their unique abilities as artists and as a reflection of their connections and problem-solving abilities. Albers broke down the disciplines in his instruction into three main categories: Drawing, Color-Painting, and Basic Design (*Werklehre*). Drawing for Josef Albers was regarded as "graphic language." He says,

> Just as in studying language it is most important to teach first the commonly understood usage of speech, in drawing we begin with exact observation and pure representation. We cannot communicate graphically what we do not see. That which we see incorrectly we will report incorrectly. We recognize that although our optical vision is correct, our overemphasis on the psychic vision often makes us see incorrectly (Albers, "Concerning Art Instruction").

In other words, before an artist can represent a "self-expression," they must understand proper unbiased sight. Therefore, the students were taught to "test" their seeing. This included a systematic study of foreshortening, overlapping, and articulation of "nearness and distance."

Albers famously tested his student's perception with the study of color. In his 1963 manual, *Interactions of Color*, Albers writes, "With the discovery that color is the most relative medium in art, and that its greatest excitement lies beyond rules and canons, a more sensitive discrimination is needed." Albers thought one should become fundamentally aware of one's way of seeing due to its relativity. This can only happen through involvement. Albers used color demonstrations to highlight the subjective dimension of color. For example, in demonstrating the reactions of a specific red shade, Albers comments, "all group members will have the same visual perception. But still the individual associations and emotional reactions will differ vastly" (Diaz 24). A demonstration such as this allows the student to track their relationship with the color beside others in the group, bringing awareness to not only the variability in opinion but also an experience in mindfulness and empathy.

Experimentation with color was just the beginning for Albers. Once the students are trained to see, they are asked to explore their process. Investigation into shape, geometry, landscape, and material followed. Each aspect is examined from this multi-tiered lens, teaching his students to have a keen awareness of their perceptions, observing them more actively through the experience and, therefore, through their art. For example, the manual act of drawing was instructed with the most basic and technical aspects in the foreground: measuring, dividing, estimating, and so on. He says, "the hand must be sensitized to the direction of will" (Albers, *Concerning Art Instruction*). The awareness of the mind to manually act, or thought to will, progresses this deep study of perception into a profound look at one's process. By excluding "expressive drawing" at the beginning of the student's studies, one can produce a distance between the object, the art, and the audience.

Albers believed that a deep understanding of the medium would lead to more apparent intentions with the student's painting process. It would also result in proper execution. For example, with paint, Albers says, "to prepare for a disciplined use of color to prevent accident, brush, or paint-box from taking authorship" (Albers, "Concerning Art Instruction"). Albers's aim was not to decentralize the artist but rather to make them experts in process and medium so that their own "authorship" would not falter at the hand of their materials. Experience with the materials becomes knowledge to make decisions and act, just as in life.

Albers blends perception with process in his explorations of the material composition of form. *Material* studies were more concerned with the technical nature and capacities of the materials. Students would test the materials by folding, bending, compressing, and stretching the medium. This resulted in a dynamic exploration of the relationships and use of objects. Through the construction process, students could then understand the economic qualities of form, such as space, volume, and dimension. This led to an active sense of balance, proportion, and composition.

Albers's focus on abstraction was rooted in *Matière* studies, which sought to explore the optical and tactile nature of things, their texture, structure, and contrasts. Students would be asked to combine found materials, remove them from their everyday context, and obscure their identities by using them in a new way. They could use a single or several different materials to create a new abstracted work. In essence, by using materials out of their standard frameworks and placing them in relationship to one another, Albers's students began to see the world around them more acutely. For example, one student, Ray Johnson, used caterpillar nests and metallic paper to create tent-like structures. When one sees a caterpillar nest in a tree, it is apparent what it is, but when paired with the reflective paper, both materials become unrecognizable.

The students would engage a hyper sense of awareness to question their perceptions, work with the materials through their process, and create a product that was an abstraction of the original through the unique lens of the student. Often, the product was activist in nature, and the artists used their art as an interaction and commentary on the world around them.

Antiracist Literacies: Activism in Action

Albers' color experiments included looking at color relationships, a skill that permeates the realm of antiracist literacy and art activism. Rather than teaching complimentary or contrasting color theories, as many art schools do, Albers would demonstrate how one's relationship with color changes depending on what other colors surround it. For example, if the particular red hue from the example above were to be placed next to lilac or brown, how would one's interaction with the color change? Does it appear to be the same hue of red, or has it somehow altered? In Eva Diaz's book *The Experimenters*, she says of Albers' instruction,

> "visual memory is amazingly poor" as compared with, say, auditory memory, and suggests that "color is deceiving us all of the time"; these influences on vision have the effect of converting "the optical (physio-physiological) susception ["stimuli'] into a psychological effect (perception)."

Because optical impressions are highly influential, the artist must be trained in perception. Training includes experience with the interaction of color and the evaluation of the resulting data from these interactions.

Albers further taught the mutability of color by exploring gradient, reverse ground, after image, color mixture, transparency, warm and cool, and many other interfaces. In each demonstration, he emphasized the shift in the reception of color based on the situation. He thought careful analysis of optical discrepancies versus their material realities could activate the student's ability to render this awareness with other habitual patterns of meaning. The artist could then become more consciously aware of their "seeing" and gain greater intuition and drive for discovery. Through experience, the student is taught that in visual perception, "there is a discrepancy between physical fact and psychic effect" (Albers 2).

Beyond the obvious application of Albers' color theory to art, Tomashi Jackson found in her studies at Yale University that his language use was strikingly similar to the use of the language of segregation in civil rights and education policy. Jackson read Albers' *Interaction of Color* alongside *Brown v. Board of Education: A Documentary History* by Mark Whitman. What she found was a stunning similarity in rhetoric. She says in an interview with *Hyperallergic*,

> The language around *de jure* segregation is similar to Albers's description of the wrong way to perceive color, as if color is static. Marshall and Albers concluded that color is relative, and what a viewer perceives a color to be is determined by the color nearest to it. Color is always changing, and, contrary to popular belief, it is not absolute. I saw the phenomenon of vibrating boundaries aligned with residential redistricting and redlining.

Jackson's insights might help us to recognize Albers' methods as "radical democracy." The implementation of her findings further these sentiments. Jackson moved to create a series of abstract paintings as metaphors for the categories of race, an exploration of process that could be equated to activism.

Albers' influence on activism endures far beyond this example. Several of his students, including Robert Rauschenberg and Ruth Asawa, went on to create organizations for arts activism. Rauschenberg famously wrote, "Art has no borders. Specialization leads to cultural sterilization. An Artist is a diplomat, a prophet, a historian, a poet, and a calendar of nourishment or morality and energy." Rauschenberg said of Albers, "[h]e didn't teach you how to *do art*. The focus was always on your personal sense of looking" (*Rauschenberg Papers*). Rauschenberg considers Albers, his most influential teacher and continues to posthumously honor his time at Black Mountain through *The Rauschenberg Residency*, which "fosters the ideal that artistic practice that advances mutual understanding and engenders a focus on the conservation of a sensitive and pristine environment and integration with the local surroundings." The foundation also offers an "Artist as Activist" fellowship, which supports artists who tackle critical social issues with a two-year grant. The program aims to serve "artists as problem solvers," a credo that mirrors Albers's mission.

Ruth Asawa founded the Alvarado School Arts Workshop in 1968, a program that involved professional artists visiting public schools to teach young children. Asawa lobbied politicians and charitable foundations for funding, scraped together found objects to use in classrooms, and eventually made her way into fifty public schools in the San Francisco area. Asawa says she was "primarily interested in making it possible for people to become as independent and self-sufficient as possible. That has nothing really to with art, except that through the arts you can learn many, many skills that you cannot learn through books and problem-solving in the abstract" (*Arts Activism*).

Conclusion: Generating Citizens and Problem Solvers

By encouraging both self-reflection and the translation of thought into action, pedagogy at Black Mountain began with art to end with democracy.

—Ruth Erickson

By the time Black Mountain went bankrupt and closed its doors in 1957, the United States was amid a critical civil rights movement. Many of the college's professors and attendees moved on to produce works of activist art, such as Robert Rauschenberg and Charles Olson, creating a sort of "opposition culture" (Duberman 433). Moreover, though the college failed to continue operation, it would hardly be considered a failure. Not only did many activist and *avant-garde* movements emerge from Black Mountain alumni, but several people moved on to learn, instruct, and influence at other higher education institutions.

Despite its lack of accreditation, graduate schools such as Harvard and Radcliffe accepted Black Mountain students based on recommendation (Duberman 101). This is not only a nod to the veneration for Black Mountain inside of academia but also a reminder that Ivy League and top-ranked institutions were at one point amongst the most progressive educators. It is apparent that the framework of higher education is being questioned as many top universities are also removing the undergraduate standardized test requirements, such as the SAT and ACT, and the graduate requirement of the GRE.

Just as Pauszek concludes in her article "Biscit" Politics: Building Working-Class Educational Spaces from the Ground Up," I want to conclude by highlighting the literacies that Black Mountain offers our sense of community literacy practices: Black Mountain provides *organization literacies* within the values and principles it used to form and operate the college. The interdisciplinary approach to the curriculum, social and cultural activities outside of the classroom, democratic methodology, and experiential learning inside the classroom give us examples of structures within a community and academic setting that operate with the goal of holistic education and citizen-making at its core. Black Mountain offers *service and collaboration literacies* as central to its foundation. Through art instruction, students have a productive problem-solving method for all disciplines and citizens while supporting the whole person with a creative outlet. Black Mountain advocates *pedagogical literacies*, as we see with Josef Albers and other educators at Black Mountain engaging in critical presence with their student's mastery of materials, introspection, and social action in the product of their labors. Finally, it left us with a legacy of antiracist literacies through the enduring influence of Josef Albers.

Higher Education has undergone several reforms in American history, in the 1930s and the 1960s. It is time to consider what was at the core of these upheavals. What is left to repair? What remains broken? Considering these examples of organizational literacies, service and collaboration literacies, pedagogical and antiracist literacies, how can we as policymakers, educators, and community members infuse these literacies into our own environments?

Black Mountain can be a window into the past and perhaps a catalyst for future advancements in rhetoric and composition, cultural studies, and beyond.

Works Cited

"Academics." *Brown University*, 23 Nov. 2022, https://www.brown.edu/academics/undergraduate/open-curriculum

Albers, Josef. *Interaction of Color*. Yale Univ. Press, 2013.

—. "Lectures" and "Texts." *The Josef and Anni Albers Foundation*, 2020, www.alberscoundation.org/.

"Arts Activism." *Ruth Asawa*, 12 Nov. 2023, https://ruthasawa.com/life/arts-activism/

Creasy, Jonathan C. *Black Mountain Poems: an Anthology*. New Directions Publishing Corporation, 2019.

Creasy, Jonathan C. *The Black Mountain Letters: Poems and Essays*. Dalkey Archive Press, 2016.

Creeley, Robert, editor. *Selected Poems Charles Olson*. University of California Press., 1997.

Dewey, John. *Art as Experience*. Putnam, 1980.

—. *Experience and Education*. Free Press, 2015.

—. "The New Era in Home and School," *John Dewey on Education: Selected writings.* New York, The Modern Library, p.11.

Diaz, Eva. *The Experimenters: Chance and Design at Black Mountain College.* The University of Chicago Press, 2015.

Duberman, Martin B. *Black Mountain: an Exploration in Community.* Northwestern University Press, 2009.

Epps-Robertson, Candace. "Teaching Must Be Our Demonstration!": Activism in the Prince Edward County Free School Association, 1963-1964. *Literacy in Composition Studies*, Spring 2015.

Kates, Susan. "Literacy, Voting Rights, and the Citizenship Schools in the South, 1957–1970." *College Composition and Communication 57.3 2006: 479–502*

Katz, Vincent, and Martin Brody. *Black Mountain College: Experiment in Art.* MIT Press, 2013.

Lathan, Rhea Estelle. "Testimony as a Sponsor of Literacy: Bernice Robinson and South Carolina Sea Island Citizenship Program's Literacy Activism." *Literacy, Economy, and Power: Writing and Research after Literacy in American Lives*, by John Duffy et al., Southern Illinois University Press, 2014, pp. 30–45.

Managed by Daphne Geismar, *Josef and Anni Albers Foundation*, 2020, albersfoundation.org/.

Mathieu, Paula. "Being There: Mindfulness as Ethical Classroom Practice," *Journal of the Assembly for Expanded Perspectives on Learning*, Winter 2015-2015, pp. 14–18.

Molesworth, Helen, and Ruth Erickson. *Leap before You Look: Black Mountain College, 1933-1957.* Institute of Contemporary Art/Boston, 2015.

Pauszek, Jessica. ""Biscit" Politics: Building Working-Class Educational Spaces from the Ground Up." *College Composition and Communication*, vol. 68, no. 4, 2017, pp. 655-683.

Puleo, Risa. "The Linguistic Overlap of Color Theory and Racism." *Hyperallergic*, 14 Dec. 2016, hyperallergic.com/345021/the-linguistic-overlap-of-color-theory-and-racism/.

Rauschenberg, Robert. *Robert Rauschenberg Foundation*, 2022, www.rauschenbergfoundation.org/.

Richards, Mary C. *The Crossing Point: Selected Talks and Writings.* Wesleyan Univ. Press, 1974.

Richards, Mary C. *Centering in Pottery, Poetry, and the Person.* Wesleyan University Press, 1989.

Rifkin, Libbie. *Career Moves.* University of Wisconsin Press, 2001.

Schneider, Steven. "The Sea Island Citizenship Schools: Literacy, Community Organization, and the Civil Rights Movement." *College English*, vol. 70, no. 2, 2007, pp. 144-167.

Schneider, Stephen. "Chapter 4: Literacy Education: Citizenship Schools and Community Organization ." *You Can't Padlock an Idea: Rhetorical Education at the Highlander Folk School, 1932-1961*, University of South Carolina Press, 2014, pp. 111–141.

Wells, Susan, et al. *Democracies to Come: Rhetorical Action, Neoliberalism, and Communities of Resistance.* Lexington Books, 2008.

Author Bio

Angela Muir is a Ph.D. student in Rhetoric and Writing Studies at Northeastern University, where her research intersects archival methods, cultural and feminist rhetorics, and contemplative pedagogy. Her collaborative work with Paula Mathieu, "Contemplative Pedagogy for Health and Wellbeing in a Trauma-Filled World," appears in Composition Studies, and her forthcoming article, "Creating Community as Contemplative Practice," will be featured in Composition Forum in Summer 2024. Beyond academia, Angela is a poet, authoring two volumes: *memory of water* (Moonstone, 2022) and *a river unraveled* (Unlock the Clockcase, 2023). She earned her BA from the University of Michigan, an MFA from Naropa University, and an MA from Boston College.

Entering the "Headspace" of Community-Based Archival Research: Reflection and Invention in an Undergraduate Community Literacy Course

Jens Lloyd

Abstract

Merging community literacy and archival research pedagogies, this article presents a qualitative study of students' reflections from a course that involves partnering with a community organization to research their archives. The article considers students' reflections about, first, learning archival methods and, second, applying these methods in a community setting. Alongside development in key areas of archival methodology, students stress the importance of sharing their research in a way that benefits the organization. The article, which is intended for teacher-scholars interested in or already involved in teaching similar courses, concludes by exploring two implications for community-engaged archival research pedagogies.

Keywords: archives, community-based learning, undergraduate research, reflection, invention

It was on a relatively mild day in March 2022 that I first brought students in my "Community Literacy and Public Rhetoric in the Archives" course to Neighborhood House. Located on a narrow, densely packed street not far from the center of Morristown, New Jersey, Neighborhood House has served residents for over 100 years. The organization's origin as a settlement house remains plainly evident in just how intimately enmeshed the physical structure is with its surroundings. On this day in March, however, I wasn't contemplating the scenery. Instead, I was focused on giving pointers to a student about how best to parallel park on the crowded street.

I was also focused on ensuring that everything for this initial site visit went according to plan. Neighborhood House is a notable community partner for my university's Center for Civic Engagement, and I didn't want to mess up that relationship. So, in the preceding days, I'd spent time coordinating carpools, mapping out the 15-minute drive from campus, and doublechecking the schedule for our visit with my contact at Neighborhood House. My students, meanwhile, were figuring out where to meet up with their carpool companions and how to manage collateral impacts to their class and/or work schedules. At the time, none of us were probably thinking all that much about what we wanted to get out of this community-based learning experience, which would involve multiple visits to Neighborhood House and to the organization's archives at a nearby public library.

I imagine this hyperfocus on logistical minutiae, especially for an initial site visit, is not uncommon for fellow teacher-scholars involved in community literacy courses. I begin with this anecdote because, in hindsight, it points to the benefit of assigning regular reflections throughout the semester. These reflections made up the bulk of the writing that students completed for the course and, thus, aided my ability to evaluate their efforts. More importantly, these reflections functioned as formative self-assessment for students. They served as what Kathleen Blake Yancey calls "constructive reflection" by facilitating for students "the process of developing a cumulative, multi-selved, multi-voiced identity" regarding their experiences in the course (14). Specifically, the reflections invited students to pause amidst the commotion and take stock of what they were learning about archival research and community literacy, two subjects that most students identified as entirely new areas of consideration in their academic lives.

During that semester, these regular reflections offered me convenient glimpses at what students were finding interesting or challenging about the combination of archival research and community-based learning. Now, a few semesters removed from the course, they provide a trove of qualitative data regarding student learning. The reflections are especially valuable because they document the step-by-step impact of our involvement with Neighborhood House as described by students themselves. In "A Convergence of Expectations: Literacy Studies and the Student Perspective in Community Partnerships," Grete M. Scott laments that evaluations of community literacy initiatives "are nearly always from the perspective of the teacher or university administrator, and the data taken from student reflective writing and course evaluations at the *end* of the semester" (85). Scott's critique suggests there are overlooked benefits to examining the formative or in-process reflections that students compose *during* the semester. While summative reflections, or the products of what Yancey deems "reflection-in-presentation" (14), are surely beneficial, they are also the places where students are likely to provide neat and tidy narratives that avoid the messy details of their learning. Following Scott's implicit suggestion, then, I am drawn to analyzing reflections composed *during* the semester because I believe they contain the more unfiltered student-generated insights about participating in a community literacy course grounded in archival research.

What emerges from the reflections is a strong indication of my students' growth as community-based, or, really, community-aware, archival researchers. The reflections confirm and, also, complicate what Wendy Hayden has observed about the benefits of archival pedagogies. In a 2015 article, Hayden argues that "it is not so much the material of undergraduate research projects but the methods used—the ways of reading, inquiry, lack of closure and easy resolutions of questions, relationship between student writers and their research—that could reconfigure how we think about a pedagogy for undergraduate research" (422). Hayden's point about the methods of archival research superseding the material can clarify what we as teachers want students to learn from courses that entail research in academic archives. But what happens when, as with my course, students breach the boundaries of academia and head into the community? What happens when we merge archival research with community literacy? Analyzing the reflections of my students, I find evidence of a more delicate balance between methods and material. Neither takes precedence when we "reconfigure" archival research for community-based learning.

Furthermore, the material of my students' research assumes a fascinating double meaning in that it refers both to the archival material they studied and to the material spaces they visited as part of the course. As my students were learning *how* to conduct archival research by tapping into the well-established body of archival scholarship in Rhetoric and Composition (Gaillet; Glenn and Enoch; McKee and Porter), they were simultaneously considering *why* their research matters to particular people and particular places. In this way, my students were enacting what Whitney Douglas terms "archival research as community literacy practice," which is challenging precisely because it counteracts the urge "[to move] archival work into academic forums" and, instead, embraces the need "to cultivate habits of mind that enable us to locate ourselves within our communities" (38). By working with members of Neighborhood House to learn its mission, understand its origin, and appreciate its contemporary service, my students were pressed to consider how their skills as rhetorically savvy archival researchers could support the organization's efforts to document and make use of its rich history.

In the next section, I describe the course and explain the reflections I assigned, which I called archival researcher journal entries. I elaborate on the point made above about the extent to which formative reflection exercises are crucial to accounting for how coursework of this sort impacts students. Then, in the subsequent sections, I analyze the archival researcher journal entries. I consider my students' reflections on, first, learning archival methods and then, second, applying these methods in a community setting. In my students' interactions with Neighborhood House, what takes on the greatest methodological importance is inventing ideas for how to share what they are learning from their archival research in a way that benefits the organization. I conclude by considering two implications for community-engaged archival research pedagogies: the binary between academic, on-campus archives and non-academic, off-campus archives and the expectations for what students—in the case of my course, undergraduates with little or no previous archival research experience—can accomplish in a semester. Ultimately, I hope my article can be used by other teacher-scholars interested in facilitating community-based archival research to foster distinctively situated learning experiences for students.

The Role of Reflection in My Community-Engaged Archival Research Course

I first taught an archival research course at Drew University in Fall 2019. At that point, the course focused entirely on research in the on-campus archives. In 2021, I was approached by the director of Drew's Center for Civic Engagement about a grant opportunity through Project Pericles, an organization that promotes civic learning in higher education ("About"). The grant offered me the chance to reimagine the archives course as one involving collaboration with a community partner, namely Cornerstone Family Programs & Morristown Neighborhood House. As explained on the organization's website, Cornerstone was founded in the early nineteenth century to serve those affected by the War of 1812. Neighborhood House was founded near the end of that same century and, according to the website, "has its roots in the Settlement House Movement [...] where leaders joined with their neighbors in underserved diverse neighborhoods to focus on reform through social justice and the fight against racial discrimination." The two organizations merged in 2013 ("Our Legacy"). The archives for Neighborhood House are held at the North Jersey History & Genealogy Center in the Morristown public library. The center recently acquired the archives for Cornerstone, but, at the time of my course, those materials were waiting to be processed. So, my Spring 2022 course was concerned exclusively with Neighborhood House, which, as indicated by its history, was its own social service entity until only very recently.

Intended for advanced English majors but open to other majors as well, the Spring 2022 course satisfied a college-wide requirement for off-campus, immersive experiences, so I was mindful about accommodating a range of students. Indeed, while most of the 13 enrolled students were English majors, the course included students majoring in History and Art History. As a teacher-scholar committed to place-based pedagogy, I was excited to provide students this opportunity to partner with an organization that plays a key role in the civic life of a nearby community. I noted in my Project Pericles grant application that I was particularly interested in asking students to focus on how Neighborhood House has supported the literacy development and community involvement of its clients. Furthermore, while there is a longstanding partnership between Neighborhood House and Drew's Center for Civic Engagement, that partnership had yet to involve archival research. Thus, the course augmented this partnership; it provided Neighborhood House with a team of archival researchers and reinforced Drew's commitment to providing undergraduates with authentic civic engagement experiences.

Regarding course content, I recognized that both archival research and community-based learning might be new for students, so I emphasized regular reflection exercises in the hopes of clarifying what students would be expected to accomplish during the semester. Reflection was the primary source of educational continuity for students. I wanted them to concentrate less on polished final projects and more on the process of acclimating to the combination of archival research and community-based learning. The reflections came in the form of archival researcher journal entries, or, more simply, ARJ entries. I informed students that these entries would be visible only to me and would provide them with the means to document their development as community-aware archival researchers. Ten ARJ entries were assigned throughout the semester with the expectation that students would write 200-400 words for each entry. I designed prompts for each entry that asked students to respond to assigned readings, record their research discoveries, and/or plan their next research steps. Readers can refer to the Appendix for the ARJ prompts and additional details about my study.

We did not start visiting Neighborhood House until the mid-way point of the semester. The first half of the course was spent reading about archival research methods in Rhetoric and Composition and conducting research in the on-campus archives, which I viewed as necessary preparation for students. During these initial weeks, I asked staff at the archives to curate selections for my students of nineteenth-century pamphlets and nineteenth- and twentieth-century periodicals. While the subject matter of the pamphlets and periodicals was generally unrelated to our eventual engagement with Neighborhood House, these materials, which derive from notable collections at Drew's archives, allowed my students to get experience with archival analysis. The first five ARJ entries document this half of the course. The final five ARJ entries document the latter half of the course when we split our time between classroom sessions, visits to Neighborhood House, and archival research trips to the North Jersey History & Genealogy Center. In contrast to their curated research in the on-campus archives, students were able to follow their interests and examine, for example, documents related to fundraising, records of volunteer recruitment, curricula for literacy programs, and plans for the construction and maintenance of Neighborhood House's facilities.

The ARJ entries showcase the active and emergent learning of my students, which can be inadequately documented and, thus, insufficiently understood by faculty in both community literacy courses and archival research courses. Scott makes this point the centerpiece of her article regarding faculty perceptions of community literacy projects: "[W]hen I asked participants about students' literacy expectations and responses to service learning, they seemed unable to give clear answers. Most of them instead told me how much their students enjoyed the service learning experience" (84). From my perspective, a cause for this is that, as faculty, our ability to perceive student learning in community-engaged courses can be obfuscated amidst other concerns such as the logistical ones I mentioned in my introduction. Furthermore, faculty reliance on end-of-semester narratives is likely to generate facile claims about student enjoyment rather than nuanced portraits of student learning. In a 2017 article, Hayden notes a related problem for archival research courses, namely that formal academic writing assigned at the end of a project does not always offer a satisfying means for students to demonstrate their learning. Hayden assigns blog entries because she "find[s] students produce better writing in the blogs than in previous analytic paper assignments that can sound stilted in their attempts to meet what they feel are the expectations of the genre." Hayden then works with students to inject the "more conversational and creative" tone of their blog posts into their "more traditional" academic writing (146). While the reflective intent of my ARJ entries mirrors the purpose of Hayden's blog entries, I did not frame them as a precursor to formal writing. Instead, echoing Yancey's terminology, I recognized the ARJ entries as "constructive" in their own right. Scaffolded over the duration of the semester, the reflection exercises helped my students make meaning out of their experiences in a community-engaged archival research course.

While it might be tempting to treat them as transparent depictions of student learning, these reflections are even more interesting to me because they are com-

Entering the 'Headspace' of Community-Based Archival Research | 35

plicated rhetorical artifacts documenting the recursive, untidy business of learning. As such, I was compelled to analyze the ARJ entries in a systematic fashion, reading them through multiple times for the sake of this study. My initial pass involved no attempts to mark or code the entries. Upon re-reading them, I developed a coding system to identify shared themes and insights. I was looking, in essence, for pieces of a common experiential narrative, one undoubtedly influenced by my decisions regarding the course structure and the ARJ prompts, but also, hopefully, imbued with students' idiosyncratic thoughts and desires. I returned to the ARJ entries for a third time to confirm that my coding system worked. Satisfied with my efforts, I noticed that ARJ #1 through ARJ #5 effectively document my students' reflections on acclimating to archival methods, while ARJ #6 through ARJ #10 effectively document my students' reflections on becoming community-aware archival researchers. Analyzing these ARJ entries is my primary focus in the remainder of this article.

Students on Reading, Connecting, and Questioning as Archival Methods

When reviewing ARJ #1 through ARJ #5, which span the first half of the semester when students were learning about and practicing archival research in the on-campus archives, what stands out it is how students articulate their growing sense of confidence as archival researchers in a manner that aligns with the common archival methods Hayden identifies in her 2015 article. To organize my analysis, I distill these methods, which Hayden lists as "the ways of reading, inquiry, lack of closure and easy resolutions of questions, relationship between student writers and their research" (442), into three overarching categories: reading, connecting, and questioning. *Reading* covers students' abilities to interpret content found in the archives, *connecting* covers their abilities to leverage their positionality as researchers, and *questioning* covers their abilities to embrace an open-ended, investigatory sensibility. The appeal of the ARJ entries is that students fashion their own language to reckon with what they are learning about archival methods. In so doing, they signal what they find important about archival research and hint at what will be foundational for their eventual engagement with Neighborhood House. For this reason, throughout my analysis of the ARJ entries, I maintain a keen concentration on students' actual words and quote extensively from their reflections to explicate their coming to terms with the three methodological categories of reading, connecting, and questioning.

An initial challenge for students was figuring out how to read when conducting archival research. Though many were English majors and, thus, had ample training in interpreting fiction and nonfiction texts, students discerned that archival methods require different interpretive moves. But this did not diminish their enthusiasm for tackling the challenge. In ARJ #3, composed about a month into the semester around the time that students were analyzing the curated selection of nineteenth-century pamphlets, Elsie writes, "I loved being able to look through documents and imagine what it would have been like to read these at the time they were published, and how the content holds up (or doesn't hold up) to modern standards." Lenny offers their own take on the interpretive moves required for archival research: "I should expect to find [my] values challenged, and perhaps even abandon, or put aside, my own be-liefs while in the headspace of archival analysis." This evocative imagery of entering a different "headspace" strikes me as a potentially disorienting shift, but that is not the case for Lenny, who, even at this early stage, has come to anticipate that reading for archival research requires temporal dislocation and a momentary letting go of con-temporary attitudes. Contrary to complaints about students' myopic interpretative tendencies, I am impressed by the power of archival methods to help students like Elsie and Lenny articulate and appreciate the benefits of contextually grounded read-ing practices.

With that said, students were also eager to connect with their archival research on a personal level. Specifically, students grappled with Cheryl Glenn and Jessica Enoch's advice that archival research is "always partial and always interested" (21). Contained in a chapter from *Working in the Archives* that I assigned at the start of the semester, Glenn and Enoch's advice regarding how to manage and even capitalize on bias was mobilized by students far more willingly than I expected. I anticipated pushback from students instructed to believe that research is only ever practiced in an objective, neutral fashion. Instead, in early ARJ entries, students cautiously embrace the advice. One student, Blythe, identifies "letting go of the idea that bias is bad" as the "most challenging aspect" of the Glenn and Enoch reading, but also accepts that one's perspective might actually "support the legitimacy" of a research project. An-other student, Remy, acknowledges that "we have our own questions and inherent biases, possibly helpful and/or harmful, which guide our research," and then offers themselves a practical tip to remember: "I will try to take note of what type of re-search I gravitate towards and see if I can expand my research to be more inclusive as well as see if the potential bias is helpful." Spending time early in the semester in the on-campus archives allowed my students to begin negotiating with personal in-terest, which, as Glenn and Enoch make clear, is something even experienced archival researchers must consider. I am glad this negotiation began in the early ARJ entries because I wanted students to have confidence about this matter, and maybe even a set of practical tips like Remy, for our research interactions with Neighborhood House.

The emotional labor of archival research was another methodological matter as-sociated with connecting on a personal level that I wanted students to confront while working in the on-campus archives. In ARJ #2, composed after my students' first for-ay into the archives at Drew, Remy and Wanda document positive experiences, with Remy noting that their "initial visit to the archives was quite thrilling" and Wanda re-flecting that they were not as "overwhelmed as [they] thought [they] would be." Con-versely, Blythe documents a negative experience that is not uncommon for archival researchers: "I found myself making upset faces at the material I had in my hands because of how these pro-slavery individuals were talking about the horrific institu-tion that was slavery." That my students were experiencing the emotional highs and lows of archival research was reassuring because, in my view, it equipped them with a degree of resolve that they could take with them into the second half of the semester. Lenny's ARJ #2 captures the ambivalence that I hoped students would learn to relish: "I had initially experienced a mixed feeling of both excitement and intimidation. My excitement was rooted in the anticipation to discover something that aligned with my interests and capability to analyze, while my intimidation was caused by the expectation to find something good and worth talking about."

This ambivalence, ideally, invites development in the third methodological category, questioning. The willingness to embrace an open-ended, investigatory sensibility begins with the thrill of novelty that students report when first immersed in archival research. "The best way I can put it," Soren writes in ARJ #1, "is it seems more dynamic than I initially thought or at least the research process is more alive. I had imagined that archival research is just like going into a library and finding a book you need [...] but the process is much more complicated." Soren's insight suggests a burgeoning appreciation for the indefinite horizons presented by the archives. In ARJ #3, Elsie elaborates on these horizons, noting "it is important to remember that each document can become a part of a different story or narrative depending on who is looking at it." Elsie, along with many peers in the course, took readily to the role of archival storyteller as described by Lynée Lewis Gaillet in her contribution to *Working in the Archives*. In response to the dearth of "codified information on archival research that we, as a profession, offer new scholars" (29), Gaillet provides a list of "tasks and questions [...for] examining data" (34). Gaillet's chapter greatly facilitated the growth of my students' confidence with archival analysis, and I think the notion of storytelling was especially appealing because, rather than feeling like they were in search of a single objective truth in the archives, students recognized they could use questioning to explore multiple subjective possibilities.

As the first half of the semester wrapped up and as we finalized plans for visiting Neighborhood House, my students expressed comfort with the inquiry-driven entanglements of archival analysis. In ARJ #5, Blythe writes, "Analysis is definitely not easy when looking at these more dated pieces [...]. However, this more mysterious element within the materials makes it more fun because I have to work in a more complex way as a researcher." This remark from Blythe is notable because, earlier, Blythe was stymied by troubling pro-slavery content in a nineteenth-century pamphlet. Yet, within a few weeks, Blythe nurtured a thoughtful approach to conducting and even enjoying archival analysis. Wanda uses ARJ #5 to generate advice they can use in the future: "I will have to remain lenient and accommodating of the differing natures of each archival visit if I want to be an optimal archival storyteller." Like Remy's practical tip about negotiating bias, Wanda's self-coaching exemplifies students rendering archival methods in their own terms and reveals the depth of learning that archival research can generate.

In this section, I have considered how my students constructed personal understandings of archival methods that, while derived from scholarly sources, are formulated to match their own experiences with *reading, questioning*, and *connecting*. How would these experiences, which up until this point were limited to on-campus archives, translate to our experiences with Neighborhood House? What would happen as my students moved from a "headspace" concerned primarily with reading, connecting, and questioning into one that also involved inventing ideas for resources that could bolster Neighborhood House's mission? I examine this in the next section by analyzing responses to ARJ #6 through ARJ #9.

Students on Inventing as a Method for Community-Engaged Archival Research

My students' ARJ entries from the second half of the semester reveal that reading, connecting, and questioning in a community setting were significantly influenced by development in a fourth methodological category: *inventing*. This category is represented at the end of Gaillet's list by the following advice: "Decide how to tell your story. What is your stance? Who is the audience? How will you organize and disseminate the findings?" (36). The fact that it concludes Gaillet's list, number eleven of an eleven-item list, signals that inventing, or thinking creatively about how to share one's findings, can arrive late in the archival research process. Yet, figuring out the story you want to tell, including details about why and to whom you are telling it, can reshape one's overall methodological approach. Inventing should be a paramount consideration for community-engaged archival research in particular because, as Douglas proposes, treating this research "as a collaborative act of rhetorical invention" encourages us to "create new knowledge and representations of that knowledge *alongside* community members" (33). Community partners can be audience members for our research, but they can also be essential interlocutors, helping us ground our stories and stances in material realities.

For my students, inventing became most palpable when visiting Neighborhood House and exploring their archives because, even more so than when we were in the on-campus archives, students found it counterproductive to maintain distanced and dispassionate perspectives. Students wanted to use their research to demonstrate their earnest commitment to serving the organization. The ARJ entries from Soren, Marty, and Blythe offer a representative portrait of what my students experienced during these weeks with Neighborhood House, so, in this section, I focalize my analysis through their reflections.

ARJ #6 was assigned after our initial visit to Neighborhood House, and some students, like Soren, quickly found a spark for their archival research through touring the physical site and talking with representatives from the organization. "I had this image of [...] a glorified daycare with parents dropping kids off when they can't take care of them during the day," Soren writes in ARJ #6, "but it was much more than that. [...] I'm most interested in how the things they offered to clients evolved, like when the services they offered grew and how that affected their retention of clients and bringing in new ones." With their expectations disrupted, Soren recalibrated their commitment to researching the organization's archives. As I will explore later in this section, Soren became quite interested in Neighborhood House's fundraising efforts.

In contrast to Soren, Marty responded to the mid-semester shift with trepidation: "This will be a far different experience than our work at the Drew archives where we had [the archivist] prepare a selection of documents for us." Marty concludes ARJ #6 by noting that they are "worried" about the research "feel[ing] overwhelming." Marty seems to suspect that our structured visits to the on-campus archives created a false sense of confidence. Yet, in ARJ #7, composed after our initial visit to the North Jersey History & Genealogy Center that maintains the Neighborhood House archives, Marty's trepidation eases as they begin the by now familiar activity of archival research: "Once I pulled out a folder [of archival materials], the process became much less daunting. Reading through the statements, budgets, and plans that I found was really exciting because it was like I was getting a glimpse into what it was like to work at Neighborhood House as it was fifty years ago." So, for Marty, getting into the comfortable habits of archival research, specifically the methods associated with reading, permits them to smooth out this transition to a different research venue.

Though following an arc similar to Marty, Blythe ultimately finds direction by contemplating invention. In ARJ #6, after visiting the site, Blythe writes: "There is so much history behind Neighborhood House [...that I think] it would be hard to narrow down my research to a few findings." Unsettled by the many possible avenues for research, Blythe's reaction following the initial site visit is a sharp contrast to Soren's. But this changes when Blythe visits the North Jersey History & Genealogy Center and begins to consider how to, in the words of Glenn and Enoch, "consciously and carefully activate the materials in the archives" (25). In ARJ #7, Blythe elaborates on this realization: "It is my job as an archival researcher to 'activate' the materials, as Glenn and Enoch say. [...] Activating is more than reading and resharing, but rather bringing a piece of history to life so that a modern-day audience can interact with it." This shows Blythe's growing confidence as an archival researcher who can make methodological adjustments by thinking creatively about sharing their findings.

Blythe's interest in sharing their findings anticipated the final assignment for the course. Drawing on Douglas for inspiration, I asked students to work on their own or in small groups to create proposals for sharing what they learned about Neighborhood House's history. In her article, Douglas describes working with colleague Eric Turley to research a famous suffragist from Nebraska and then using their findings to support a community organization that was producing a touring theatrical performance about voting rights (30-31). Douglas' article reflects upon and theorizes this "generative community literacy practice" (31), and it presented my students with a model for thinking creatively about what they could offer to Neighborhood House as community-aware archival researchers. In addition to encouraging creativity, I had my students read Heidi A. McKee and James E. Porter's "The Ethics of Archival Research," which relies on interviews with prominent archival researchers in Rhetoric and Composition, to consider how personal motives can be both valuable resources and necessary restraints for inventing. In the section of their article about motives, McKee and Porter assert that "[p]ersonal interest in pursuing a line of inquiry is, of course, a vital starting point for any successful project, but 'because I am interested in ...' should not represent the entirety of your rationale for purpose and motive" (64). McKee and Porter pose questions for archival researchers to consider, one of which seemed the most consequential for my students: "Does what I am doing or planning to do have value and benefit beyond my personal interest and, if so, to whom?" (65). Reckoning with the "value and benefit" of what could be done with archival research did not put a damper on my students' inventing; rather, it added a dose of practicality to how they sought to enact their roles as community-aware archival researchers.

Students started to brainstorm ideas for their final assignment in ARJ #8 after reading and discussing Douglas' article. Soren, who researched Neighborhood House's finances and recognized how vital fundraising was to the organization's efforts to promote literacy and community involvement, considered cataloging past fundraising initiatives to offer ideas for future ones. Marty speculated about digitizing important organizational documents like meeting minutes and annual reports to make them easily accessible to the executive leadership and the staff at Neighborhood House. Blythe, who researched the role of volunteers, saw the potential to compose a report outlining the popular motivations for volunteering at Neighborhood House in the hopes of helping the organization attract and retain a large cohort of volunteers.

Following this brainstorming, I asked students to use ARJ #9 to reflect on how their understanding of motives via McKee and Porter could enhance their proposals. The responses for ARJ #9 were the lengthiest of the semester, signaling students' interest in this aspect of their research. Soren's motives again indicate the significance of visiting the site: "[My research] started really as just an assignment for this class, but after we went for our first visit it made me realize how important this organization was for the community and I got pretty invested in it. [...] I think that this organization means so much to so many people that keeping it well funded would be very important." Marty and Blythe were more influenced by personal connections. Marty explains: "I grew up around childcare. My mother has run a preschool and kindergarten program on the first floor of our house for more than 20 years. So, I've been exposed to programs similar to that which Neighborhood House offers my whole life." Meanwhile, Blythe notes: "Even though I was born and raised in the US, my parents immigrated here from Colombia. In this way, I have been exposed to both cultures and have been able to learn what it is like to immigrate to this country. This is why I am so thankful for and interested in Neighborhood House's work." With McKee and Porter's discussion of motives a clear influence on their thinking, these students maintain a subjective stake in their research while brainstorming creatively about how their research can benefit the organization.

With the final assignment, I asked for fully developed proposals rather than fully realized projects because of the constraints imposed by the semester. My students, many of whom began the semester with no archival research experience, did not have the time or the means to bring their projects to fruition. Is this a satisfying end for an undergraduate course that merges archival research and community literacy? Also, what about the implicit and, admittedly, unintended bifurcation of academic and non-academic archives generated by the structure of my course? In the concluding section, I consider these implications, beginning with the latter.

Implications for Community-Engaged Archival Research Pedagogies

In ARJ #10, the final reflection, I asked students to write about something they learned in the final weeks of the semester that they wish they had learned earlier.

Marty offers a perspective that, when I first read it, cast a momentary shadow over the entire enterprise of merging archival research and community literacy:

> Getting hands-on experience in both the place we're researching and the archives that houses their documents was a really useful experience. It changed my perspective from that of an outsider, simply reading about archival research, to actually doing it myself. We did have our trips to the Drew archives earlier in the semester, but those felt further removed from the subject matter we were researching.

To me, Marty's end-of-semester appreciation for "hands-on experience" is a necessary companion to Lenny's evocative "headspace" imagery from ARJ #3. After all, this "headspace" is never entirely in one's head; there is always a material component. Archival research always happens some*where*. What is perplexing, though, is that there was a material component to the early weeks of the semester when we left our classroom to visit Drew's archives. But, for Marty, this on-campus research generated a feeling of being "removed from the subject matter," of scrutinizing things from a safe scholarly distance.

On one level, Marty's comment confirms the benefits of community-based learning and indicates that archival research means something different when you can become, following Marty's logic, an insider by exploring the material site that is the subject of your research. On a more critical level, Marty's comment suggests that my course reinforced the binary between academic and non-academic settings. This binary is, as Donna M. Bickford and Nedra Reynolds insist, an enduring issue for community-based learning experiences that, by focusing on activities beyond the campus, "may simply reinforce the notion of the ivory tower for [students] or lead them to believe that, while the community may need their services, the university does not" (244). I think this explains the ideology at work in Marty's comment. For Marty, researching in Drew's archives seemed less real because the campus was not framed as the site in need of archival researchers. Neighborhood House was framed as the site in need, and this was conveyed, albeit unwittingly, in the way I structured the course.

The implication for community-engaged archival research pedagogies is that we ought to address this binary directly with students. One possibility is to elucidate for students, where possible, the links between the campus and the community. For instance, as I noted, Drew's Center for Civic Engagement has a history of partnering with Neighborhood House. Helping students recognize their roles in continuing this history could circumvent the issue that Bickford and Reynolds identify. Furthermore, the Neighborhood House archives presented opportunities for researching deeper historical ties between the organization and the university. In ARJ #8, Lenny writes about finding archival documents that describe the volunteer efforts of Drew students in Neighborhood House's Sunday School. Though Lenny did not follow this Drew-specific research trajectory, it could be something I showcase in the next iteration of this course. While I would not require students to focus on Drew-specific research, showing them that such trajectories exist could help to undermine the imagined barriers between their campus and the community.

The other implication I want to address in this conclusion regards expectations for what can be accomplished by undergraduates in a course that blends archival research and community-based learning. Elegant examples of fully realized projects from courses like mine can be found, such as Erin Brock Carlson's place-based work with her students in West Virginia. But, because my course aimed both to introduce students to archival research methods and to get them implementing these methods in a community setting, I felt it unrealistic to expect fully realized projects. I did not want to rush my students through the acquisition of skills in reading, connecting, and questioning nor did I want them to hastily conclude their research. Instead, by focusing on invention, my course emphasized what Jacqueline Jones Royster and Gesa E. Kirsch define as "strategic contemplation" in that it asked students "to withhold judgment for a time and resist coming to closure too soon in order to make the time to invite creativity, wonder, and inspiration into the research process" (85). Lingering with invention resonates not only with strategic contemplation but also with the ongoing, unfinished nature of archival research. I believe that, based on my analysis of students' ARJ entries and my experience teaching the course, invention was a meaningful culmination of student learning. Sticking with proposals allowed invention to stand as a substantial milestone on its own, signaling to Soren, Marty, Blythe, and others that inventing can be, and perhaps needs to be, an intense but rewarding phase of community-engaged archival research.

Still, because the proposals remained a class assignment and were never formally shared with Neighborhood House, my students arguably missed out on experiencing the full effect of inventing with/in the community. To remedy this, when teaching the course again, I could add a session where students share their proposals with Neighborhood House representatives, get feedback, and then submit a revised proposal. Those proposals the organization finds exceptional could be mobilized and supported outside the parameters of a college course. A model for this approach is described by Jeanne Law-Bohannon and Shiloh Gill Garcia in their contribution to a recent collection about archival pedagogies. Law-Bohannon and Garcia explain how, supported by a donation from a private foundation, "a pilot class assignment" evolved into a multifaceted initiative "that collects oral history [...] and complementary artifacts" about the Civil Rights activism of the Atlanta Student Movement and "then curates them in a digital collection" (264). Another remedy could involve introducing students to the broader range of writing that supports and enables archival research. I could derive a model for this approach from Jonathan Buehl, Tamar Chute, and Laura Kissel's contribution to the aforementioned collection about archival pedagogies. Promoting the idea of "archives as professional writing spaces" (180), Buehl, Chute, and Kissel remind us that archives are sustained by many genres, including publicity materials and grant proposals (182-184). Students in a future version of my course could write for and about the Neighborhood House archives rather than Neighborhood House itself, which might end up benefiting both the organization and the North Jersey History & Genealogy Center that maintains the organization's archives. I prefer the latter approach because students could work dynamically with multiple community partners to brainstorm strategies for preserving the history of an organization that has contributed so much to civic life in a campus-adjacent community. It would reinforce collaborative invention as a worthwhile phase of community-engaged archival research, worthy enough of being the end for my particular course.

Though they might have ended the course without fully formed projects, students did arrive at fully formed conclusions about the impact of participating in this community-based learning experience. "When we visited Neighborhood House," Elsie explains in ARJ #10, "it was great to see the ways that they have evolved over time without having to go through physical documents, though that was helpful in my research. I appreciated the human aspect of the learning we have done in this course, as we were able to talk to people who have worked in Neighborhood House and can tell us real accounts of their experiences." Clearly, for Elsie, though interest in Neighborhood House was bolstered by research in the archives, it was neither limited to the archives nor did it necessarily originate there. While interested in Neighborhood House's past, Elsie was just as interested in learning about and supporting the organization's present and future. To this point, on our final visit to Neighborhood House, I recall Elsie stopping by the front desk to ask for information about volunteering for the organization during the upcoming summer break. This anecdote serves as a fitting conclusion for this article because it signals that, while students can accomplish quite a lot *during* a course that merges archival research and community-based learning, what matters as much as anything is what students consider doing with their time and energy *after* participating in such a course.

Acknowledgments

I wish to thank the staff at Neighborhood House, especially Holly Dinneny, and the staff at the North Jersey History & Genealogy Center, especially James Lewis. I'm grateful for the support of Project Pericles and Drew's Center for Civic Engagement. I'd also like to acknowledge Candace Reilly, Manager of Special Collections at Drew, who guided my students through their initial archival endeavors. Speaking of the students, I appreciate their efforts and insights, and I'm proud that their words shine most brightly in this article. Lastly, I dedicate this article to Maureen A.J. Fitzsimmons, a friend and grad school colleague who got me thinking about archival research in the first place.

Appendix

Details about the study: Eleven out of the 13 enrolled students consented to have their ARJ entries collected for my IRB-approved study. To maintain confidentiality, when I cite the entries in this article, I use pseudonyms and they/them pronouns. On a lark, I had ChatGPT generate random pseudonyms to add another layer of confidentiality. My analysis of the ARJ entries started once the course ended. I gathered them electronically from our learning management system and assembled them in separate documents, one for each numbered ARJ entry.

Prompts for the ARJ entries:

ARJ #1

For this first entry, reflect on your initial experience in this course. From reading the syllabus to exploring *The Drew Acorn* during our first meeting, from reading the *Working in the Archives* excerpts to exploring the "Silva Rhetoricae" website during our first full week, what have you learned about archival research in writing and communication studies?

Some questions you might consider: What stands out to you, and why? What are you looking forward to, and why? What confuses you, and why? What might be challenging and how might you mindfully tackle these challenges? Be specific and reference our readings and activities as necessary.

ARJ #2

Tell me about your initial visit to the archives for our course. How was it? What did you find? What garnered your interest, and why?

Beyond that, address one or more of the following:

- Review the list of tasks on pages 35-36 in Gaillet's chapter. Which of those tasks have you done? What haven't you done? What do you still want to do, and why?
- Review the steps outlined on the prompt and consider where you're at in terms of completing the pamphlet analysis. In the words of Glenn and Enoch, what do you think you need to do to "activate" the material you've found?

ARJ #3

Address one or more of the following questions:

- What did you learn from the pamphlet analysis about being both an archival analyst and an archival storyteller?
- If you had an extra day to dedicate to the pamphlet analysis, what would you do with that extra time, and why?
- What did you learn from listening to your peers during the show-and-tell?

ARJ #4

Tell me about your initial visit to the archives for the periodical analysis. How was it? What did you find? What garnered your interest, and why?

Beyond that, address one or more of the following:

- Consider the lessons you learned from the pamphlet analysis. How can you take those lessons and apply them to the periodical analysis?
- Review the list of tasks on pages 35-36 in Gaillet's chapter. Which of those tasks have you done? What haven't you done? What do you still want to do, and why?
- Review the steps outlined on the prompt and consider where you're at in terms of completing the pamphlet analysis. In the words of Glenn and Enoch, what do you think you need to do to "activate" the material you've found?

ARJ #5

Address one or more of the following questions:

- What did you learn from the periodical analysis about being both an archival analyst and an archival storyteller?
- If you had an extra day to dedicate to the periodical analysis, what would you do with that extra time, and why?
- What did you learn from listening to your peers during the show-and-tell?

ARJ #6

Tell me about your experience during our initial visit to Neighborhood House.

Consider addressing one or more of the following questions:

- What did you learn about Neighborhood House that most interested you?
- What aspect of Neighborhood House's history (including the many different types of services it has offered to clients over the years) are you most interested to explore, and why?
- What challenges do you anticipate in studying archival materials related to Neighborhood House?

ARJ #7

Tell me about your initial visit to the North Jersey History & Genealogy Center. How was it? What did you find? What garnered your interest, and why?

Beyond that, consider addressing one or more of these questions:

- Review the list of tasks on pages 35-36 in Gaillet's chapter. Which of those tasks have you done? What haven't you done? What do you still want to do, and why?
- Consider what you did for the pamphlet analysis and periodical analysis. How might your previous experiences in this course help you with researching the Neighborhood House archival materials? In the words

of Glenn and Enoch, what do you think you need to do to "activate" the materials you've found?

ARJ #8

Tell me about your second visit to the North Jersey History & Genealogy Center. How was it? What did you do to build on the research you did last week? What do you still need to learn about the Neighborhood House materials you've been studying?
   Beyond that, consider addressing the following:

- Inspired by Douglas' account of her community engagement project, what do you think you could do with the archival materials you've studied in order to promote and publicize the history of Neighborhood House?
- What are you most interested in sharing with our community partners at Neighborhood House when we return next week, and why?

ARJ #9

Tell me about the ethics of the archival research and community engagement project that we're undertaking with Neighborhood House.
   Specifically, consider your motives by addressing one or more of the following questions (which I've adapted from pages 64 and 65 of McKee and Porter's article):

- What are your motives for conducting this research involving Neighborhood House? How do your background and experiences shape the questions you're asking and the conclusions you might draw?
- Why is it important on a personal level for you to research Neighborhood House? Does what you're studying have value and benefit beyond your personal interest and, if so, to whom?

ARJ #10

Reflect on your work over the last few weeks and your visits to Neighborhood House and the North Jersey History & Genealogy Center. What have you learned that you wish you had known earlier about being an archival researcher involved in a community-based learning project?

Works Cited

"About." Project Pericles, www.projectpericles.org/overview.html. Accessed 18 June 2023.

Bickford, Donna M., and Nedra Reynolds. "Activism and Service-Learning: Reframing Volunteerism as Acts of Dissent." *Pedagogy* 2.2 (2002): 229-252.

Buehl, Jonathan, Tamar Chute, and Laura Kissel. "Professional Writing for the Archives: Collaboration and Service Learning in a Proposal Writing Class." *Teaching Through the Archives: Text, Collaboration, and Activism*, edited by Tarez Samra Graban and Wendy Hayden, Southern Illinois UP, 2022, 178-193.

Carlson, Erin Brock. "'I Have Always Loved West Virginia, But...': How Archival Projects Can Complicate, Build, and Reimagine Place-Based Literacies." *Community Literacy Journal* 17.2 (2023): 25-48.

Douglas, Whitney. "Looking Outward: Archival Research as Community Engagement." *Community Literacy Journal* 11.2 (2017): 30-42.

Hayden, Wendy. "'Gifts' of the Archives: A Pedagogy for Undergraduate Research." *College Composition and Communication* 66.3 (2015): 402-426.

Hayden, Wendy. "And Gladly Teach: The Archival Turn's Pedagogical Turn." *College English* 80.2 (2017): 133-158.

Gaillet, Lynée Lewis. "Archival Survival: Navigating Historical Research." *Working in the Archives: Practical Research Methods for Rhetoric and Composition*, edited by Alexis E. Ramsey, Wendy B. Sharer, and Barbara L'Eplattenier, Southern Illinois UP, 2010, 28-39.

Glenn, Cheryl, and Jessica Enoch. "Invigorating Historiographic Practices in Rhetoric and Composition Studies." *Working in the Archives: Practical Research Methods for Rhetoric and Composition*, edited by Alexis E. Ramsey, Wendy B. Sharer, and Barbara L'Eplattenier, Southern Illinois UP, 2010, 11-27.

Law-Bohannon, Jeanne, and Shiloh Gill Garcia. "Is Anyone Sitting Here?: Mirroring Gaillet's 'Survival Steps' in a Community-Based, Justice-Focused Classroom." *Teaching Through the Archives: Text, Collaboration, and Activism*, edited by Tarez Samra Graban and Wendy Hayden, Southern Illinois UP, 2022, 263-278.

McKee, Heidi A., and James E. Porter. "The Ethics of Archival Research." *College Composition and Communication* 64.1 (2012): 59-81.

"Our Legacy." Cornerstone Family Programs and Neighborhood House, cornerstonefamilyprograms.org/about-us. Accessed 18 June 2023.

Royster, Jacqueline Jones, and Gesa E. Kirsch. *Feminist Rhetorical Practices: New Horizons for Rhetoric, Composition, and Literacy Studies*. Southern Illinois UP, 2012.

Scott, Grete M. "A Convergence of Expectations: Literacy Studies and the Student Perspective in Community Partnerships." *Community Literacy Journal* 5.1 (2010): 75-89.

Yancey, Kathleen Blake. *Reflection in the Writing Classroom*. Utah State UP, 1998.

Author Bio

Jens Lloyd is an Assistant Professor at Drew University, where he also currently serves as Director of First-Year Writing. Specializing in composition theory and pedagogy, Jens has a particular interest in place-based approaches to research and teaching. You can find some of his scholarly writing in *Rhetoric Review, Literacy in Composition Studies,* and *Reflections: A Journal of Community-Engaged Writing and Rhetoric.* He also contributed a chapter to *Bordered Writers: Latinx Identities and Literacy Practices at Hispanic-Serving Institutions,* an edited collection that received the CCCC Advancement of Knowledge Award in 2021.

Issues in Community Literacy

Section Editor's Note: This piece was delivered as part of the zoom-based "Issues in Community Writing Dialogue" series hosted by the Virginia Community and Public Writing Collaborative and sponsored via a 4VA grant.

"How Community Means"

Donnie Johnson Sackey

Abstract

These brief remarks delve into the essence of community as purposeful connection. Through collaborative design interventions, it explores what it means to build relationships within communities in pursuit of environmental justice. The author shares his experiences from two research projects, which offer insights for community-based researchers dedicated to social transformation.

Keywords: community-based research, issues in community writing, collaborative-design interventions

The title of my opening remarks is "How Community Means." For me, *to mean* denotes having a purpose. I have always been interested in the creation of technical interventions that facilitate better relationships between people, their communities, and environments. The creation of these interventions has been the result of design work—broadly conceived—and has been a collaborative process in which I have had the privilege to collaborate with communities, center their concerns, needs, and hopes, and build things. The predicate for my title is to emphasize how we can continue to assemble and create opportunities *with* communities in pursuit of change and justice through design. What I'd like to do is briefly talk about two community-based projects that center design as a primary concern, offer you a sense of what I've learned, and perhaps portend what work we all might collectively accomplish as community-based researchers interested in literacy.

Moment no. 1: Understanding Food Insecurity & Designing for Security

In 2019, Dawn Opel and I had the opportunity to partner with the Food Bank Council of Michigan to make sense of data-driven approach to food insecurity. The Michigan Legislature uses a series of data products that help them determine resource allocation for food assistance throughout the state. They tracked pounds of food distributive throughout the state's pantry network and visualized that the result in the form of a map. Dawn and I knew that the story of food insecurity (and food security) could not be told in terms of pounds of food distributed. We knew that we had to move beyond the seductive quality of data visualizations" and attend to the "dangerous implications for research quality, and the human subjects represented" (Hepworth p. 7-8). To truly understand how food insecurity manifests, we had to work with end-users of the pantry system—particularly a group of people who have little opportunity to design the data-driven tools (e.g., policies, software, data visualizations) that form the thorny thicket that prevents them from moving beyond a state of precarity. Central to our work was to ascertain how the interaction between design techniques and the community characteristics of end-users' influence data-collection, policymaking, and access to social services (e.g., Supplement Nutrition Assistance Program (SNAP) benefits, housing assistance, etc.); and devise how can we approach the design of databases and data visualizations from a bottom-up rather than top-down perspective, so that they capture the complexity of users' experiences rather than reducing them to discrete data points. Our conversations with staff and clients from two pantries revealed the need to rethink the definition of "food insecurity" to purposefully collect information that was often excluded at the point of the client intake process, because we fail to value people's expertise in the things they know the best—their own experiences.

Moment no. 2: Designing for Larger Participation in Water Governance

Since 2015, part of my ongoing work in Flint, MI has been to work with a group of community activists who formed an ad hoc group, which communication researchers and disaster sociologists refer to as emergent organizations, as they work to become "more cohesive and unified during situations of collective stress" and are "more innovative in resolving their problems and more resilient in the wake of severe challenges than they are given credit for" (Drabek and McEntire p. 99). Within the discipline of crisis communication, we rarely privilege the voices of those affected by emergent crises, choosing instead to favor issues of management, locating information, how and when information circulates, and whether information is accurate and useable. My work with this group has largely focused on what might happen if we were to amplify those voices. And perhaps, how can we, as researchers, go a step further by building mechanisms for more participation around water governance in communities to avoid the kind of crisis we saw in Flint. Our work has been to think creatively about what kind of resources can be developed to improve the community's resilience and also hold officials accountable. Some of this work has centered on the design of consumer confidence reports (CCRs).

CCRs, sometimes called "Annual Drinking Water Quality Reports," are federally-mandated documents that summarize information about the local drinking water for the previous year. CCRs emerge because of amendments to the 1996 Safe Drinking Water Act (SDWA), which created the "right to know" more information about community water systems. In theory, CCRs help to raise consumer awareness of where their water comes from; inform consumers of the process by which their water is delivered; educate consumers about water safety; and allow consumers to make more informed decisions regarding their drinking water. As important as these documents are, their design is heavily under researched. In fact, CCRs design have been influenced by the perspectives of engineers, scientists, and government regulators. These perspectives have led researchers and community advocates to argue that CCR's design alienate a public that has very little scientific literacy in a time when scientific literacy is more important than ever. Water crises from Flint, Michigan to Pittsburgh, Pennsylvania to Jackson, Mississippi have created a heightened sense of risk regarding the safety of our water systems. These crises have also created a heightened interest in citizen participation in water governance. Improving public participation in water governance necessitates designing good tools that can support citizens' contribution to deliberative processes. And this is currently what I'm doing as part of this group. We've endeavored to think about how a redesign of CCRs might allow for greater participation.

Each of these projects have centered empathy, creativity, iterative learning, and improvement in the pursuit of environmental justice. At their core, they recognize and contend with the latent impact of maleficent design—or what Rob Nixon refers to as "slow violence." However, in each of these opportunities, I've spent a lot of time meditating on what it means to be useful. In this regard, I've been motivated doubly by Jeffery Grabill's call for rhetoric researchers to pay attention to the knowledge work people are doing in the commonplaces of their lives and to consider expansively what larger facilitative roles we can play; as well as William Hart-Davidson's call of "Why not us?"—a call for technical & professional communication specialists to play more agentive roles in the design of the technologies that people interact with in the everyday.

I've learned many things in the process of these projects but what sits with me most are a set of provocations (or perhaps opportunities) and guiding questions that I think we might all collectively meditate upon.

Provocation #1: Changing the Model of When and How Community-based Research Happens

How can researchers shift from traditional researcher-led research design models to co-creation research models that centers community research concerns and actively involves community members as equal partners in the research process?

Considering the resource disparities between universities and community partners, what strategies can be implemented to build the capacity of community members to meaningfully contribute to research initiatives and ensure equitable collaboration?

I've been thinking a lot across projects about what we are doing to show communities that we are available and that the spaces of universities and colleges are theirs just as much as ours. And that they have the capacity to do research that can affect change in their lives. In thinking about my project with the Food Bank Council, it should not take a group of researchers to recognize and explore a problem that members of a community are familiar on account of their everyday experiences. I'd like to see us build centers and research clusters in which community members bring problems to institutions and make community members a part of your research team. I've had the opportunity to create a couple of these ad hoc clusters, but I think that we can a should create more research opportunities like this. Part of this initiative involves moving from a researcher-led research design model in favor of a co-creation research model in which community research concerns lie at the center and all parties are seen as researchers. Much of the work we can do to facilitate this process is building the capacity of community members to actively participate in research initiatives. This requires investment in training, education, and skill development to support community members to contribute meaningfully to the research process. This might also require the development of resources within communities, so that they can do research on their own terms. Universities have greater access to funding, equipment, and institutional support compared to the community partners which who we collaborate. This resource disparity can create barriers to meaningful collaboration and limit the capacity of community members to fully engage in the research process.

Provocation #2: Avoiding Crisis-Driven Community-Based Research

How can researchers shift their focus from crisis-driven narratives to exploring and understanding community resilience in their community-based research endeavors?

How can we ensure that community-based research is conducted in an ethical and empowering manner that avoids potential harm and exploitation?

For a lot of researchers, community-based research that involves disaster and ruin is extremely compelling. I think that's a problem. Research in Flint has really opened my eyes to the way in which community-based research that emerges as the result of crisis can be predatory and perhaps do more harm than good. In the weeks after the Flint water crisis emerged, there was a seemingly endless torrent of researchers trying to establish research projects within the city. Perhaps this is why I've been reticent to publish on Flint. I found that more people were interested in reading about why *I* was doing in Flint and how that fit in *my* progress to tenure and promotion, which all paled in comparison to things I was encountering in Flint. I think that the Flint Water Crisis should remind us of the dangers of the top-down research model in which concern and expertise emerge from outside the community. In this moment, I felt less interested in being a researcher with respect to what I could offer the discipline and how I could benefit from that. And more interested in what I could offer the community. I think that everyone in here will agree that we will always benefit more than the communities with whom we collaborate. But I think we can get so mired in doing research that we ignore a larger duty of care that asks us to be humans first and researchers second. Researchers like Eve Tuck, Laura Gonzales, and Cana Uluak Itchuaqiyaq have urged us to move beyond damaged-based research even if our intentions emerge from a space of benevolence. Top of FormIf we can choose to see communities like Flint in crisis, we can also choose to see these communities as resilient. Such a turn-in-phrase is a look toward imaging communities like Flint—post-crisis or outside the frame of crisis entirely. Suspending crisis-driven research and centering our research around community resilience promotes empowerment, reduces stigmatization, builds trust, and enhances psychological well-being.

Works Cited

Drabek, Thomas, and David A. Mcentire. "Emergent Phenomena and the Sociology of Disaster: Lessons, Trends and Opportunities from the Research Literature." *Disaster Prevention and Management*, vol. 12, no. 2, 2003, pp. 2003.

Gonzales, Laura. *Designing Multilingual Experiences in Technical Communication*. Logan: Utah State University Press, 2022.

Grabill, Jeffery T. "The Work of Rhetoric in the Common Places: An Essay on Rhetorical Methodology." *JAC: A Journal of Composition Theory*, vol. 34, no. 1, 2014, pp. 247-267.

Hart-Davidson, William. "On Writing, Technical Communication, and Information Technology: The Core Competencies of Technical Communication." *Technical Communication*, vol. 48, no. 2, 2001, pp. 145–55.

Itchuaqiyaq, Cana Uluak. "No, I won't Introduce You to My Mama: Boundary Spanners, Access, and Accountability to Indigenous Communities," *Community Literacy Journal*, vol. 17, no. 1, 2022, pp. 97-99.

Hepworth, Katherine. "Big Data Visualization: Promises & Pitfalls." *Communication Design Quarterly*, vol. 4, no. 4, 2016, pp. 7-19.

Nixon, Rob. *Slow Violence and the Environmentalism of the Poor*. Cambridge: Harvard University Press, 2013.

Tuck, Eve. "Suspending Damage: A Letter to Communities." *Harvard Education Review*, vol. 79, no. 3, 2009, pp. 409-427.

Author Bio

Donnie Johnson Sackey (he/him) is assistant professor in the Department of Rhetoric & Writing at the University of Texas at Austin where he teaches courses in environmental communication, information design, user-experience design, and nonprofit writing. He serves on the steering committee of the Polymathic Scholars Honors Program and the Bridging the Disciplines Smart Cities faculty panel. His research centers on the dynamics of environmental public policy deliberation, environmental justice, and environmental community-based participatory research. He is a non-resident fellow with the Center on Global Energy Policy's CarbonTech Development Initiative at Columbia University. His research has appeared in *Communication Design Quarterly, Community Literacy Journal, Present Tense, Rhetoric Review, Technical Communi-*

cation Quarterly, and various edited collections. He is also the author of *Trespassing Natures: Species Migration and the Right to Space* (Ohio State UP, 2024).

"Inviting the Body": Walking Methodologies as a Process of Unlearning

Jamie Crosswhite

Abstract

This article delves into an exploration of the transformative journey of integrating walking methodologies within the context of a Technical Writing in the Community service-learning course, which is offered at a Hispanic Serving Institution (HSI) located in south Texas. These walking methods, founded on the principle of engaging the physical body in the learning experience, serve as a dynamic conduit for building bridges between the academic sphere and the broader non-academic communities that surround it. In the wake of the COVID-19 pandemic, which significantly altered the educational landscape, there has been a growing recognition of the need for innovative approaches to education that prioritize equity and inclusivity. This article places particular emphasis on the concept of "unlearning" as a central tenet of this experiential pedagogical practice. The act of unlearning challenges entrenched and conventional structures within education, offering a powerful means of fostering meaningful change. In an era marked by heightened awareness of issues related to equity, diversity, and inclusion, as well as the ongoing call for decolonization within educational institutions, the integration of walking methodologies takes on added significance. This article explores how these methods can play a pivotal role in reshaping the educational landscape, helping to break down barriers and create more inclusive spaces for learning. Acknowledging that no pedagogical approach is without its challenges and limitations, the article concludes by underlining the importance of persistently inviting the body into the process of learning and unlearning through the use of walking methodologies. It calls for a continued exploration of these innovative techniques as part of a broader effort to cultivate more responsive and equitable educational experiences. By embracing the transformative potential of walking methodologies, educators and institutions can move closer to the goal of fostering a more inclusive and equitable educational landscape.

Keywords: walking methodology, service-learning, unlearning, technical writing pedagogy

Introduction

I started the spring 2023 academic semester by asking the students in my Technical Writing in the Community course to *unlearn* their stationary outlook of the writing process. I wanted them to move beyond the bounded expectations of writing as a seated practice achieved strictly in front of a computer screen or settled at a desk with pen and paper. Unlearning invited students to consider their body as the center for writing, and offer their writing skills, products, and time as a form of service. Students were urged to think of the nuanced ways that words and composition could be shared, could make change, and could be a reciprocal tool for learning. One of the practices incited to support unlearning in our Technical Writing classroom was to take up walking as an essential part of this process. I encouraged students to walk, wander, and write outside the box of our enclosed classroom and travel beyond the margins of their Word documents and power-point templates. We used walking methodologies as a way of unlearning traditional writing practice and engaging in community literacy through experiential learning, though not without complication.

Legacy of Social Justice Grounded in Place

As Nedra Renalds, Gloria Anzaldúa, Jenny Rice, and others have affirmed, place matters, especially in relation to intersections of learning, writing, and identity. As we write and teach and create and learn, we are sowing a future that is grounded on the legacies and shortcomings of those who worked the land, composed the literature, and educated the generations before us, calling this same place *home*. We stroll the halls and trample the soil others toiled to harvest. The institution where I work, where my students learn, and the city that surrounds us, harbor a legacy of service, social justice, and the intrepidity to take risks, sometimes for the betterment of others and sometimes not. I teach at Our Lady of the Lake University (OLLU), a small Catholic liberal arts school in San Antonio, Texas. OLLU was founded by a group of strong women in 1895. Mother Florence Walter, the superior general of the Sisters of Divine Providence, looked out over the land where our university now sits and asserted: "This is the place. Someday, upon this land will stand a beautiful Gothic chapel with twin spires pointing up to the blue Texas sky" ("OLLU History"). Her vision has become reality, though there is still work to be done in acknowledging the destructive role of settler colonialism and exploitation of indigenous peoples and land in creating the city of San Antonio and our university. Historically and presently, there are complexities and conflicts grounded in questions of settlement and service.

The Sisters of Divine Providence were initially established in San Antonio to educate rural communities beyond the city's reach as well as serve the westside of San Antonio, a part of the urban landscape troubled with social injustice, systemic oppression, and limited access to municipal services. The sisters' first educational ventures required them to travel, sometimes on foot, to serve those who otherwise would not have access to education. Many of these communities were poverty stricken, and women and people of color dealt with additional social and educational barriers and violences. These early narratives of the institution are oversimplified in our university archives, online history, and in conversations across our campus and community. The founding sisters are often depicted as *saviors* to these *lost* communities. Challenging and scrutinizing these uniquely documented origins is arduous for students and faculty, particularly in the presence of living faith-oriented individuals who inhabit our campus spaces and learning environments, and with institutional values and vision profoundly rooted in faith-based principles. A potential avenue for further inquiry and analysis is the exploration of counterstories in subsequent endeavors and iterations of this course. However, based on the existing documentation, the sisters' educational initiatives expanded, and the college was established.

In 1986, OLLU became the birthplace of the Hispanic Serving Institution designation or HSI ("OLLU: The Birthplace of HSI"). Dr. Antonio Rigual, OLLU's provost, assembled a group of leaders from eighteen universities to openly discuss the founding of an association of colleges and universities that served substantial populations of Hispanic students. From that meeting, the Hispanic Association of Colleges and Universities (HACU) was established and was housed on the OLLU campus through its early years. Working from this foundation, OLLU maintains its HSI status, and continually assesses and explores how to best serve our students and community. There are divergences and disputes on how to implement this HSI obligation in a pragmatic manner. Faculty and administration frequently hear that we are "sitting on the shoulders of giants," which is an uneasy position to occupy in ambiguity. We are assigned with exceedingly high criteria for service to students, community, and university, resulting in our research and other interests being allocated scant time and resources.

The heritage of our place at Our Lady of the Lake University is one of assisting our immediate community as well as a mindfulness and action-oriented education focusing on the specific population of students we serve; however, one-hundred-twenty-seven years after the founding of our institution, systemic oppressions and injustices continue. There remains a passion towards community literacy and social justice, but these are not always executed efficiently or effectively. Students in my Technical Writing in the Community course engaged with the legacy of our common place and its complex history, as well as its imperfections and bias. One approach students were prompted to recognize both merits and drawbacks was by unlearning conventional writing practice through walking methods, situating their own body in this place and knowledge production, thereby contemplating on positionality and process.

Unlearning

Measuring student learning is a difficult task, and measuring unlearning is perhaps even more arduous. Unlearning is defined as the process of replacement or disuse of knowledge, action, or procedure and substitution of new knowledge when appropriate (Hafner 2015; Hedberg 1981; Starbuck 2017). As outlined by Moshe Banai (2022) and Hislop et al. (2014), most studies of unlearning have been within the framework of organizational structures and practices, but the theory has been applied to cultural assimilation, educational leadership, and learning exercises. The theory of unlearning asks for a shift in methods and practices for individual or structural change, despite cultural and institutional limitations.

The praxis of unlearning within a formalized educational system is paradoxical; however, unlearning can be practiced as a way of pushing against standardized education structures embraced by the majority that marginalize those not equipped with a privileged background. As part of a blog series on social justice and civic engagement, Dr. Jin Young Choi, explains the significance of unlearning as it relates to privilege and oppression. She defines what it means to unlearn as an act of "discarding or nullifying what we have learned when it is wrong, false, or outdated; to forget your usual way of doing something so that you can learn a new and sometimes better way" (Choi). Post-Covid education with lingering health and equity concerns, as well as decolonial and DEI driven education initiatives, insist that institutions and instructors unlearn what is false or outdated, and seek a new and sometimes better way. The students in my Technical Writing class were asked to forget their usual way of writing and include walking as an integral part of the process. Within the confines of a semester, students incorporated experiential education practices of centering the body and movement into the writing process. Several students reflected and voiced how they gained confidence through this approach and tried incorporating walking methods within other classes as well as their personal writing and creative projects. The question remains if unlearning will stick, if it will transcend my request in a single semester to make change. More studies, reflections, and student feedback are needed, but the initial student experience in the spring 2023 semester revealed a shift in writing practice and signs of unlearning through this experiential effort were successful.

Somatic Pedagogy/Walking Methodologies

Although academics often acclaim achievements of the mind, the cognitive labor, the indicators of intellect and innovation, the body is the site of all learning, writing, and research. The work of the mind is not so easily separated from the body. Largely, people recognize how their body influences their mental discernments and physical pursuits, but few reflect on the body's role in learning. While some may have fervent body awareness in social or health related frameworks, as part of adopting somatic pedagogy and for a deeper level of knowledge, the body must be overtly integrated with the particular subject students are expected to learn. Somatic pedagogies, such as walking methods, should be considered as a viable means to knowledge making and a way to bridge academic communities with non-academic communities. Service-learning is an excellent site to build this bridge since the two communities are already in conversation.

At the Adult Education Research Conference in 2008, Tara Horst argued that "the key to fostering somatic learning is to overtly include the body as part of the learning. The body should be actively invited into the learning space" (Horst). Walking as an essential part of the writing process and means to understanding the community invites the body into the learning space. The body is acknowledged and embraced as an essential tool in the process. Instead of clinging to the tendency to classify learning as either mental or physical, we should create room for modes of learning that are embodied, unlearning the dominance that is cultivated by constantly praising and promoting only the cognitive learning paradigms. Adrienne maree brown argues in *Pleasure Activism: The Politics of Feeling Good* that somatics is a change method to help us engage in bodied change; it is a means of reclaiming our bodies for social analysis and systemic transformation. Walking methodologies is one way to do this work.

Sarah Truman and Stephanie Springgay conceptualize walking methodologies in *Walking Methodologies in a More-Than-Human World* as a corporeal approach that scholars and students employ to investigate sensory, material, and transient aspects. Although walking as a methodology has a historical background in social critique and urban analysis, in contemporary practices it provides an embodied research method and pedagogical instrument that fosters student involvement with place, a means to unlearn or defamiliarize the spatial realities that students may not deliberately discern or scrutinize otherwise. This methodology enables students to comprehend the role of body and place in writing, identity construction, community development, and language, by eliciting a tangible, affective awareness of place(s) that cannot be fully grasped or valued in the abstract. My Technical Writing in the Community service-learning course served as a venue where the somatic pedagogy of walking methodologies was applied. Students were invited to walk with their community partner and throughout our shared community to better understand audience.

In practice, the positionality of my students, myself, and our community was crucial. As an able-bodied white female educator and researcher, I must be aware of my own prejudice and blind spots; I have to take into account how my students may perceive walks similarly or differently from my own walks, and I have to create space in my classroom for these dialogues. We examine social positionalities of walking while being Black, brown, female, undocumented, or differently abled. We investigate what walking looks and feels like on our campus and community, as well as other locations across the city. Students are encouraged to share their stories. We discuss the specific spaces they will be required to walk through as part of our class; students are free to ask questions, express their concerns, or consult with me individually. In subsequent iterations of this course, I intend to broaden these conversations on walking and positionality to explore national and global commonalities and differences. San Antonio and OLLU are distinctive and complex in their minority majority communities and stratified histories; students may gain from exploring perspectives and narratives that intersect, complement, and challenge their viewpoints.

Walking Methods Meets Service-Learning

Much like social relationality while walking, service-learning is fraught with questions of power, positionality, and privilege. Though first acclaimed as an excellent pedagogy for civic engagement, a number of researchers and theorists have signaled that the potential in service-learning for transformative change may instead unintentionally reinforce or even strengthen power imbalances (Boyle-Baise, 1999; Cross,

2005; Himley, 2004; Hullender et al., 2015; Sleeter, 2001). One strategy to address and confront these systems of power is a shift from traditional service-learning to critical service-learning. As originally coined by Tania Mitchell, critical service-learning should aim to dismantle systems of oppression. Santiago-Ortiz outlines the goals of traditional service-learning as "student-focused and outcomes-based," she addresses how this "vision has been challenged for reinforcing unequal power dynamics, engaging with community issues superficially, and providing temporary solutions that do not address oppressive conditions" (44). Similarly, Harkins et al. define critical service-learning as "a model that adopts a social justice framework, as opposed to a more 'apolitical helper' model of service-learning and demands an analysis of power structures and social change" (22). Though service-learning remains flawed, a critical approach works to assess, acknowledge, and expose inequities. As Himley argues, service-learning should "agitate us," for it is a "complex process of proximity and distance," but we should "not give up on community service learning (or debates about the 'right' way to do it)" (433).

Each semester at OLLU, there are courses that are designated and designed as service-learning sections. Our Center for Service-Learning and Volunteerism collaborates with faculty, students, and community partners to attempt to implement critical service-learning. OLLU has enduring relationships with the non-profit organizations it partners with to try to prevent power dynamics, perceived savior complexes, and to facilitate students through the process and provide them with a voice. Naturally, there are shortcomings and flaws, and some semesters are more successful than others. I will persist in reevaluating and examining what worked and what did not, what to eliminate and what to retain, and I will involve students and our community in these dialogues. Currently, the organizations we serve are part of the same community as the university, and many of our students originated from this shared neighborhood. We strive for respect and reciprocity, motivating students to recognize what they contribute and what they receive.

Prior versions of Technical Writing in the Community necessitated students to produce technical documents for non-profit organizations that lacked the resources or personnel to create, revise, and disseminate these materials. Students devised, composed, and refined deliverables such as slick sheets, organization handbooks, reports, manuals, web content, and brochures for community organizations to utilize. Communication between students and the community transpired predominantly through digital means. In the initial version of Technical Writing in the Community, service-learning was only enacted through document production for non-profit organizations, creating a disconnection, a gap between students and the purported community they were supposed to serve. Students fulfilled the mandatory tasks but did not distinctly comprehend document production as service. Their work was mainly conducted on campus, in the confines of the classroom, on a computer screen. Their bodies were not explicitly welcomed into the learning space.

Transitioning to Somatic

In spring 2023, I adopted a more somatic approach that incorporated walking. I incorporated a two-hour general service component that instructed students to walk the facilities of the non-profit organization and serve the needs of the community by opting for one of several embodied service alternatives. Some students opted to assist in creating a legacy garden, others contributed to a town hall meeting, and a few undertook more personalized tasks as specified by our community partner. Subsequently, students were prompted to reflect on these embodied experiences and the majority articulated how they felt more connected by walking, not only to the organization they were serving, but also to their classmates, and the technical written assignments they executed from campus. By mandating a minimum of two on-site general service hours and an initial site visit where students would walk-with to physically explore the facilities of their non-profit organization, students and community partners would walk and learn together, foregrounding the body as part of this process. This shift entailed walking the premises of the non-profit organization and the adjacent community.

The day I announced this walking requirement as part of the service-learning, students were not enthusiastic. They rolled their eyes, they averted their gaze, they groaned, and two students approached me right after that specific class session to express their apprehensions. Walking was not how they envisioned technical writing skills, nor was it part of their usual knowledge making process. Nevertheless, throughout the progression of the semester and through their walking practices, their attitudes changed and all but one student persisted. They worked at unlearning their prior conception of writing as a sedentary act and broadened their view of service to encompass composition.

The class was divided into three teams and each team traveled and walked together. Students designated a communication liaison for each group who scheduled their site visits; all three teams arrived on their prospective days. Our community partner for the semester was a non-profit blood and tissue bank that has been serving the greater San Antonio region for over forty-five years. Most students were unfamiliar with the organization even though it is not far from our institution and hosts blood drives on campus every fall and spring. During their site visit, students walked through the facilities of the organization they would serve in the months to follow. They met with an administrative leader, a research scientist, a graphic designer, an onsite volunteer, and others working in various departments. As students walked the halls, they were struck by the community created art installations that lined the walls and the recycled cans that were hung decoratively from the ceilings creating a sense of shifting skyscapes. As they walked into various offices and labs, they talked to individuals who expressed a sense of familial closeness within the organization and outlying community. Students witnessed blood draws, and one student nearly fainted upon seeing the storage of gallons of community blood to be disseminated throughout our region to those in need. Teams walking the grounds *with* the community partner built a stronger connection than previous iterations of this course.

In addition to walking with the community partner, students were asked to take their ideas for a walk as they created each deliverable. As part of the writing process, I urged students to walk and incorporate movement, especially when they felt stuck, when they felt the words and ideas weren't flowing, they should simply move, wander, walk, acknowledging their body is an essential tool for writing. During these walks, students were encouraged to think about their time with the community partner, their audience, as well as the larger community they were serving with their writing and beyond it. This experiential effort was an act of unlearning, and at first students were skeptical. I assured them these walks were a way to connect the knowledge and expertise they had been acquiring in the classroom and from their textbook, from the technical writing skills to the understanding of audience, to the community that their audience and they were simultaneously serving through this process. Community, writing, body, and service were intimately connected.

At the end of the course, students organized a showcase of learning and reflection where the community partner was welcomed to attend and provide feedback on their final products before delivery. Students narrated their experiences and anxieties and spoke proudly about the technical documents they produced, but they dwelled on their onsite service experience and how they felt establishing rapport with the community partner through walking and tactile engagement. I observed subtle differences in the ways students articulated their experiences compared to previous semesters. I could discern they had a more robust understanding of audience, and their final documents manifested this profound understanding by being more elaborate, more vivid in their depictions. Walking methods fostered a process of unlearning that incorporated the body into the educational and community space, connecting the two even if precariously. Reflecting on the semester, I should have asked students to supply documentation or visual evidence, such as photographs, within their reflections to more explicitly demonstrate how walking was part of their process and how they specifically perceived and felt it in action. This is an aspect of the pedagogy I will concentrate on enhancing this coming spring, but I am confident that walking methods in conjunction with service-learning offered students a distinctive educational experience that stimulated change.

Conclusion

Subsequent versions of Technical Writing in the Community as well as incorporating walking methods into other classes will uncover a more refined understanding of this experiential education practice, but from my spring 2023 experience I can affirm that unlearning through walking methods was a worthwhile risk. It was not, however, a smooth transition. Throughout the semester there were communication errors, disruptions in schedule due to freezing weather conditions, and irritations related to transportation difficulties. As an instructor I had to be adaptable and adjust to challenges I had not previously anticipated in more classroom-oriented course structures. Students and community partners also encountered new difficulties in this process. There were definitely constraints. I anticipate each new semester will generate its own issues and triumphs. I acknowledge that more attention, research, and application must be devoted to discussions about able-bodiness, and the manifold ways we walk, move, and wander our shared places and educational spaces, and the concealed or controversial histories upon which they are constructed. The body, however, should continue to be invited into the learning and/or unlearning process, and walking methodologies welcome such conversations.

Works Cited

Anzaldúa, Gloria. *Borderlands: The New Mestiza/La Frontera.* 3rd ed., Aunt Lute Books, 2007.

Banai, Moshe. "Toward a General Theory of Expatriates' Cross-Cultural Adjustment." *International Studies of Management & Organization,* vol. 52, no. 1, 2022, pp. 25–43.

Boyle-Baise, Marilyn. "'As Good as It Gets?' The Impact of Philosophical Orientations on Community-Based Service Learning for Multicultural Education." *The Educational Forum (West Lafayette, Ind.),* vol. 63, no. 4, 1999, pp. 310–321.

Brown, Adrienne Maree. *Pleasure Activism: The Politics of Feeling Good.* AK Press, 2019.

Choi, Jin Young. "Unlearning Privilege and Oppression." Blog Series: Social Justice and Civic Engagement, 6 Aug. 2020, http://www.wabashcenter.wabash.edu/2020/08/unlearning-privilege-and-oppression/.

Cross, Beverly E. "New Racism, Reformed Teacher Education, and the Same Ole' Oppression." *Educational Studies (Ames),* vol. 38, no. 3, 2005, pp. 263–274.

Hafner, J. H. "Computer System Unlearning in Individuals." Paper presented at the 48th Hawaii International Conference on Systems Science, Kauai, HI, 2015.

Harkins, D. A., et al. "Building Relationships for Critical Service-Learning." *Michigan Journal of Community Service Learning,* vol. 26, no. 2, 2020, pp. 21–37.

Hedberg, Bo. "How Organizations Learn and Unlearn." In *Handbook of Organizational Design,* edited by Paul C. Nystrom and William H. Starbuck, Cambridge University Press, 1981, pp. 3–27.

Himley, Margaret. "Facing (Up to) 'the Stranger' in Community Service Learning." *College Composition and Communication,* vol. 55, no. 3, 2004, pp. 416–438.

Hislop, Donald, et al. "The Process of Individual Unlearning: A Neglected Topic in an Under-Researched Field." *Management Learning,* vol. 45, no. 5, 2014, pp. 540–556.

Horst, Thomas. "The Body in Adult Education: Introducing a Somatic Learning Model." *Adult Education Research Conference,* 2008.

Hullender, R., et al. "Evidences of Transformative Learning in Service-Learning Reflections." *The Journal of Scholarship of Teaching and Learning,* vol. 15, no. 4, 2015, pp. 58–82.

Mitchell, T. D. "Traditional Vs. Critical Service-Learning: Engaging the Literature to Differentiate Two Models." *Michigan Journal of Community Service Learning,* vol. 14, no. 2, 2008, pp. 50–65.

"OLLU History." *Our Lady of the Lake University.* http://www.ollusa.edu/about/history.html

Reynolds, Nedra. *Geographies of Writing: Inhabiting Places and Encountering Difference.* Southern Illinois University Press, 2004.

Rice, Jenny. *Regional Rhetorics: Real and Imagined Spaces.* Routledge, 2014.

Santiago-Ortiz, Ana. "From Critical to Decolonizing Service-Learning: Limits and Possibilities of Social Justice-Based Approaches to Community Service-Learning." *Michigan Journal of Community Service Learning,* vol. 25, no. 1, 2019, pp. 43–54.

Sleeter, Christine E. "Preparing Teachers for Culturally Diverse Schools: Research and the Overwhelming Presence of Whiteness." *Journal of Teacher Education,* vol. 52, no. 2, 2001, pp. 94–106.

Springgay, Stephanie E., and Sarah E. Truman. *Walking Methodologies in a More-than-Human World: WalkingLab.* 1st ed., Routledge, 2018.

Starbuck, William H. "Organizational Learning and Unlearning." *The Learning Organization,* vol. 24, no. 1, 2017, pp. 30–38.

Author Bio

Jamie Crosswhite is an Assistant Professor of English at St. Mary's University in San Antonio, Texas. Her research encompasses several critical areas: place-based rhetoric(s), where she explores how our surroundings shape communication and influence the way we express ourselves in writing; critical regionalism, where she delves into the unique characteristics of specific regions, investigating how local culture, history, and geography impact communication practices and identity formation; intersectional identities and place, where she examines how intersections of identity—such as race, gender, and socio-economic status—shape experiences and narratives within the spaces we inhabit; and feminist studies, where she critically analyzes gender dynamics, representation, and agency.

Identifying a Gap in Prison Literacies: The Needs of Formerly Incarcerated Sexual Offenders

David Kocik, Casey O'Ceallaigh, Kayla Fettig, and Maria Novotny

Abstract

Community literacy and writing scholarship have been central to advancing disciplinary commitments to prison literacy and teaching within prison systems. Yet, within this field, little scholarship has applied prison literacy work to issues encountered by those who are formerly incarcerated. This article responds to that gap and outlines new exigencies for prison literacy scholarship to tend to the complex literacies required of those *formerly* incarcerated. Specifically, we focus on the challenges of formerly incarcerated sexual offenders who served time in prison yet remain in 'perpetual punishment' as they are mandated to navigate life outside of prison yet remain surveilled by the national sexual offender registry. We contend there are new literacies required to navigate life as one ages while formerly incarcerated, and that these literacy needs are particularly amplified if one ages while still required to be listed on the registry. This study summarizes a community-engaged graduate seminar project that introduced us to the complex literacies needed to navigate the eldercare system after incarceration while registered as a sexual offender. Our work leads us to call for community-engaged scholars to consider the literacy needs of oft-ignored prison populations: those in need of eldercare and those on the sexual offender registry. We conclude with a call for prison literacy scholars to consider how the lack of access to critical digital literacies continue to perpetuate inequities and injustices even after inmates leave incarceration.

Keywords: prison literacy, incarceration, eldercare, the registry, sexual offenders, reflection

Introduction

In the spring of 2021, David, Casey, and Kayla enrolled in Maria's "Community Literacies & Writing" graduate seminar course at the University of Wisconsin-Milwaukee. For the three of us, the topic of community literacy and community writing was rather new. Each of us had varying degrees of experience not only collaborating with communities for teaching and/or research, but we also had not been exposed to many of the theories and concepts central to the field of community literacy and writing. For Maria, this was a new course as well. While she had not yet taught a course focused explicitly on this area of study, she had a range of experience collaborating with community partners for a variety of academic-related projects. The lessons she had learned through her collaborations (Novotny and Gagnon; Novotny et al.), served as a foundation to design the seminar as an 'experiential learning' course where the class would work collectively on a literacy-based project related to incarceration.

At our first class, Maria expounded upon her decision to ground our seminar in experiential learning by sharing how she had developed a community-based partnership with a Milwaukee-based organization referred to as "The Community." The Community was founded by a formerly incarcerated person, "Robin", who was working to create educational programming across the state to "correct the narrative" around persons who were formally incarcerated. Maria had previously collaborated with Robin and The Community in the fall of 2021 with a technical editing course. As that course and collaboration ended, Maria shared Robin had approached her with a new and more "complex" project that could benefit from student engagement. She shared that the project focused on the lives of those formerly incarcerated, specifically those on the sex offender registry. Further complicating the project, Maria shared that these sexual offenders no longer in prison faced a new hurdle: accessing eldercare and the ability to research and find assisted and/or nursing care facilities that would accept them while still being listed on the registry. This task – researching and identifying the various literacies required for aging sexual offenders to find acceptable eldercare – would be our experiential learning project, Maria announced.

The remaining time during that class was spent reflecting on and openly discussing this project and the unique and rather uncomfortable challenges it presented. First, many students had little experience with the field of community literacy and writing, particularly prison literacies. Second, and perhaps most unsettling, was the fact that the project required collaborating with formerly incarcerated sexual offenders and situating their needs as a subject warranting social justice action. Collectively, these two parameters posed a unique set of challenges for the class and Maria to overcome. As such, in the following weeks, Maria structured the course to tap into these uncertainties. We researched and familiarized ourselves with issues connected to life upon release from incarceration, registering as a sexual offender once released from prison, and the challenges posed in accessing eldercare outside of prison.

Our class's research led us to an alarming reality: the prison population in the US has been aging for several decades, placing immense pressure on health and eldercare systems in and outside of prisons (Carson and Sabol; McKillop and Boucher). As prisoners and formerly incarcerated individuals age, complex legal and healthcare systems make finding sustainable care incredibly difficult for these populations. Elder or end-of-life care can be hard to secure, as eldercare living facilities often have stipulations against formerly incarcerated people, even those who have completed their parole. Although public health, mental health, and law scholars have tackled these issues, relatively little work in prison literacies has considered how an aging prison population affects how we approach and engage in our work. This essay takes up that gap and puts forward the claim that community-engaged and prison literacy scholars can provide a vital new perspective to the intersections of eldercare and the prison industrial complex. Specifically, we reflect on the web of literacies needed for aging registrants to secure eldercare. In detailing the unique literacy needs of formerly incarcerated persons, we see an ample need for community writing and literacy scholars to develop community-engaged literacy projects which may help prisoners build literacy skills and use literacy tools to find care when *outside* prison walls. By tracing the various and emerging literacy needs of those living "in the shadows" of incarceration, we hope this piece inspires other community-engaged scholars invested in criminal justice reform and advocating for prisoner rights.

Surveying the Field of 'Prison Literacies'

Engagement with issues connected to criminal justice reform, critical prison studies, and prison literacy has grown over the past decade in community literacy and writing scholarship (Barrett; Bower; Castro and Brawn; Curry and Jacobi; Erby; Hutchinson; Lockard and Rankins-Robertson; Middleton; Rogers). Prison literacy scholarship has contributed to shifting academic discussions about where and for whom literacy matters — beyond classroom walls and into the confines of prison. For instance, Tobi Jacobi's (2016) work advocates for a radical transformation of "the ways we think about and relate to the millions of people locked up in the United States" (71). Documenting the use of curation to encourage storytelling and exploration, Jacobi's work offers an innovative intervention into not just accessing stories of injustice but understanding and developing connections to issues pertinent to criminal justice reform. Similarly, Patrick Berry's (2017) research urges community literacy scholars to revise previously held notions about where and for whom literacy matters. His ethnographic account of incarcerated students' uses and understanding of literacy's power in and out of prison "challenges polarizing rhetoric often used to define what literacy can and cannot deliver" but also puts forward "more nuanced and ethical ways of understanding literacy" (3) for incarcerated persons. Collectively, Jacobi and Berry's work has facilitated connections between the prison system and writing, rhetoric, and literacy studies.

Community literacy scholarship, like that of Jacobi and Berry, offers evidence that higher education can and should contribute to issues of prison reform by advancing opportunities for educational access within prisons and has led to other scholars adopting more critical stances to prison literacy abolition initiatives. For example, Anna Plemons' (2019) autoethnographic monograph deploys a decolonial framework to critique emancipatory approaches to prison literacy and writing project. For Plemmons, the use of decolonial theory can be an asset to disrupting "the colonial impulse that uses individual narratives of transformation to measure the efficacy and value of prison education programs" (10). Similarly, Alexandra Cavallaro (2019) also finds it necessary to engage in a critical theoretical framework to critique prison literacy programs. Drawing on queer theory and critical prison studies, Cavallaro urges writing and literacy scholars "to intervene in the project of citizenship production by challenging and critiquing the logics of individualism that underwrite prison literacy programs" (3). And, more recently, Rachel Lewis (2020) draws on their experience as a member of a LGBTQ+ prison abolition community to consider how power differentials play out in prison abolition work and the circulation of prison letters in abolition newsletters. Emerging from her analysis, informed by queer theory, is the importance of relationships amongst marginalized inmates, like those who identify as LGBTQ+.

We share these examples of scholarship as they have been pivotal in advancing the work and potential of what community literacy and writing scholars can offer to criminal justice reform at-large, particularly as federal aid becomes available to incarcerated persons. That said, we note that little attention has focused on the impact of life post-incarceration. For us, our collaboration with Robin and The Community revealed a great need for careful attention to the unique literacies needs of those who may be formerly incarcerated but remain system impacted. In fact, sexual offenders released from prison are some of the most marginalized in prison literacy work. Many remain in "incarcerated limbo" a term we use to refer to those who are no longer living in prison but remain monitored by the prison system. This term helps us understand the unique literacies required of living as a person no longer in prison but who faces limits on their life because of their criminal history. For those who are sexual offenders, the barriers to access to basic care and needs are significant and something our class came to understand more personally as we worked with Robin and a formerly incarcerated sexual offender in our graduate seminar course.

Literacy Needs while Aging on the Registry

In the US, the "registry" is a euphemism for a complex system run by state and federal governments that monitors and tracks the whereabouts of sexual offenders, providing information about their names, current locations, and past offenses to authorities and the public. By collecting sexual offenders' private information, the "registry" serves as a national database, alerting citizens to the presence of sexual offenders in their communities and maintaining surveillance over released inmates. Prison justice advocates have argued that while the "registry" is described by law and policy makers as a database serving the safety and best interests of community members, all too often it operates as a form of "perpetual punishment" where those on the registry are still regularly monitored, despite having served their sentences.

Mandates to be listed on the registry and the duration of listing depend on the severity of the sexual offense and local jurisdictions. Most sexual offenses are handled through state courts, but sexual offenders convicted of particularly severe crimes must be listed on the national sexual offender registry. According to the Adam Walsh Child Protection and Safety Act of 2006, sexual offenses are divided into three tiers based on severity. Depending upon the tier of offense, sexual offenders must be listed on the national sexual offender registry. For those offenders who are older and/or who must register for life, additional challenges may be encountered, especially when seeking assisted living and end-of-life care. Locating facilities that accept sexual offenders can be difficult and may depend on federal funding.

Older offenders and those required to register for life face additional challenges, especially when seeking assisted living or end-of-life care. For example, assisted living and nursing homes that accept Title 19 funding (Medicaid) cannot house individuals on the registry. Finding housing and proper medical care for elderly registrants often requires many literacies, including digital, health, and prison literacies. Many aging registrants who have been released receive little help to find care and do not have the technological literacies needed to navigate complex digital databases on their own. Although newsletters, pamphlets, and, increasingly, digital technologies have entered some of the prison systems in the US, many elderly registrants still do not know how to access information about care facilities after release. For those required to be listed on the registry, finding a suitable home often necessitates internet access, the ability to navigate housing and health care databases, and effective communication between parole officers, registrants, social workers, and eldercare facility staff.

Developing a Database of Eldercare Facilities for WI Registrants

These three points of intersection (access to housing, access to healthcare, and living as an aging registrant) are where our class project enters the conversation. We first met and began collaborating with "Avery," a former sexual offender who had approached Robin about the need Avery's friends, who were aging registrants, had to locate eldercare housing. Avery joined our class through Zoom in the middle of the semester. He shared that he was currently working on identifying and developing a database of eldercare facilities for formerly incarcerated persons required to remain list as sexual offenders in Wisconsin. Avery disclosed to us that many formerly incarcerated persons, especially those on the registry, often rely upon each other's post-incarceration experiences to navigate life upon release. As a registrant himself who also relied on these networks, Avery saw how many formerly incarcerated, and often elderly, sexual offenders needed additional assistance due to the various literacies required for life post-incarceration. This included navigating Wisconsin's online eldercare facility database and understanding the criteria for Title 19 funded assisted living facilities. Over Zoom, Avery posed to our class the idea of creating a database of eldercare facilities that might accept aging registrants along with a tool kit to teach use of the database. The database would need to be regularly updated, maintained, and shared with parole and probation officers, social workers, and registrants in the state.

In Zooming with Avery and learning more about the personal stories and challenges many of his friends were facing in finding eldercare housing, the class began to strategize and develop a plan of action to build a database that featured eldercare facilities that might accept people on the sex offender registry. In particular, we believed it necessary for the database to serve aging registrants with fewer digital and health literacy skills and to help them more successfully navigate the complexities of the eldercare system. Initially, searching the publicly available Wisconsin registry and collecting addresses of registrants to identify those living in eldercare facilities seemed straightforward. We quickly learned, however, that calling all 3,000+ eldercare facilities in Wisconsin alone was impractical. To increase our efficiency, the class drew on our skills in Excel and internet navigation to compile a database of likely eldercare facilities in the state. As we found potential facilities, we compared the addresses of people on the public sex offender registry with the addresses of eldercare facilities in Wisconsin, both of which were available, but hard to find, on Wisconsin state government websites. If an address of an eldercare facility matched with someone on the sex offender registry, we marked it as a potential match. After sifting through these databases twice over several months, we identified about 230 facilities in the state that matched with individuals on the registry. Along with the Excel database, we created a tool kit that explained how to use the database. We then shared the database with Robin and Avery at the end of the semester, who became the managers of the database because Robin and Avery had connections with case workers, parole officers, and other registrants in need of eldercare.

With the database assembled, our part in the community project was over and Robin and Avery shared the database with other registrants, prison wardens, and case workers in the state. The database was a much-needed resource for these stakeholders as it helped them avoid the complexities of searching digital databases or calling and outing themselves as registrants to eldercare facilities. However, long waitlists at health care facilities were still difficult to navigate. Because they were in such demand, the facilities that the formerly incarcerated registrants attempted to seek healthcare from often became or were already full. With fewer options for eldercare facilities, registrants had to be put on waitlists for only a few facilities, severely impacting their access to needed eldercare. Although our collaborative project established a working database of possible facilities, the lack of eldercare of any kind made it even more difficult to find the necessary care for those on the registry. Our project with Robin and Avery gave these registrants resources to refer to in their search for eldercare, but the perpetual punishment by the prison system was still hard to overcome.

Reflecting on New Needs, New Challenges for Prison Literacy

A central goal that guided our decision to write about this course project and share it with readers of *CLJ* is to reimagine the potential for prison literacy scholarship and interrogate assumptions embedded in abolitionist work. As readers will note, this was a very different approach to a graduate seminar class and a course that also offered a different take on teaching and overviewing "traditional" prison literacy or prison writing scholarship. For these reasons, we believe it is important to share how we found this course experience and collaboration helpful in identifying additional areas where community literacy and writing scholars can contribute to issues facing prison impacted persons. First, our project focused on working with people often not discussed in prison literacy work, including people on sex offender registries, formerly incarcerated people, people on parole, and aging populations. As we continue working with prison-affected populations, it's important we understand how not all incarcerated individuals encounter the same barriers to access. Laws vary by state and local jurisdiction, and incarcerated people are affected by different stipulations from inside and outside the prison industrial complex. We understand that working with sexual offenders is particularly difficult for academic researchers for several reasons.

First, such work puts scholars in close contact with sexual offenders, which may trigger negative emotions and experiences for all parties involved with the production and circulation of such work. Second, scholars may fear harassment for working with issues of sex and sexual crimes in an academic environment hounded by conservative norms for work on sex, sexuality, gender, and sexual crimes. While these are legitimate concerns, we also argue that the barriers of parole, the registry, and stipulations in the eldercare system put intense pressure on this population. Our project only scratched the surface of the overlapping barriers that people on sex offender registries face, and we believe prison literacy scholarship might grapple with a broader variety of prison experiences, even those that are uncomfortable.

Next, our work calls into question how we as scholars might envision and enact prison literacy projects, specifically the lack of work on digital prison literacies. Community-engaged scholars have discussed the powerful experiences of sustained literacy programs focused on reading and writing within prisons, but these kinds of traditional literacy programs often become the de facto conception of what constitutes prison literacy work. Our project varies widely from these programs. Our community partners were a prison advocacy organization and an individual on the registry, rather than a prison. The project also focused much more on digital literacies, like navigating government databases and cross-referencing data, than more commonly considered literacies like reading and writing. Our community partners did not have the time, resources, and digital literacy skills to navigate the complex and obtuse registry and eldercare facility databases. So, the expertise we offered stemmed from our abilities to navigate digital spaces effectively, skills that many within the aging population do not have. While the barriers to reading and writing literacies are a major impact on the lives of incarcerated people, we urge prison literacy scholars to consider how digital literacy skills, including effective search strategies and website navigation, can supplement the critical literacies already being addressed.

Along the same lines, we call on prison literacy scholars to consider how the aging of the prison population may impact our ongoing work. As these populations age, common health issues like hearing loss, cognitive decline, and technological difficulties make it difficult for prison-affected groups to find the care they need. Prison literacy programs can address these concerns by developing and maintaining reading and writing literacy skills for aging prison populations. Literacy skills development and retention programs can equip individuals with strategies to navigate the prison system as they age. Programs can also develop resources for aging populations, such as the eldercare database we developed. These resources could simplify searching for care, and partnering with technical writing and health writing programs could provide much needed support. Working with prison populations to develop these resources could further help aging prisoners to develop skills in health system navigation.

Finally, prison literacy scholars should continue to discuss how our work fits with the needs and experiences of formerly incarcerated populations that still feel the effects of the prison industrial complex. Literacy programs within prisons often work with discrete populations of prisoners that are easy to bring together. Formerly incarcerated populations are much more difficult to work and establish relationships with as they leave the confines of prison. Yet, these individuals often need help with developing and maintaining literacy skills, particularly skills needed to navigate the complex health care system in the US. Prison literacy programs could work with parole officers or prisons to develop methods of working with formerly incarcerated people directly, and these programs could focus on developing skills necessary to read, navigate, and understand the overlapping health care and prison systems.

As we look to new horizons in prison literacy scholarship, we ask: What do we as teachers, researchers, and advocates do to understand the growing challenges of formerly incarcerated people seeking eldercare after they leave prison? How can we imagine new potentials for what these projects can do with/for prison literacy and the communities we work with? We urge community-engaged scholars to continue advocating for and working with prison populations while considering how digital literacy skills and aging prison populations challenge our assumptions about the literacies and populations we work with.

Works Cited

"Adam Walsh Safety Act." *Justice.gov*, May 2005, www.justice.gov/archive/olp/pdf/ag_guidelines.pdf.

Amidon, Timothy R., et al. "Community Engaged Researchers and Designers: How We Work and What We Need." *Communication Design Quarterly*, vol. 11, no. 2, July 2023, pp. 5–9. doi:10.1145/3592356.3592357.

Barrett, Larry et al., "More than Transformative: A New View of Prison Writing Narratives." *Reflections*, vol. 19, no. 1, 2019, pp. 13–32. https://reflections-journal.net/wp-content/uploads/2019/08/Reflections-19.1-Barrett-Mendoza-Middleton-Rubio-Stromblad.pdf.

Berry, Patrick W. *Doing Time, Writing Lives: Refiguring Literacy and Higher Education in Prison*. Southern Illinois University Press, 2018.

Bower, Stephanie et al., "The Truth Will Set You Free: Reflections on the Rhetoric of Insight, Responsibility, and Remorse in Rhetoric for the Board of Parole Hearings." *Reflections*, vol. 19, no. 1, 2019, pp. 79–112. https://reflectionsjournal.net/wp-content/uploads/2019/08/Reflections-19.1-Mo-Bower-Raymond-P.-Artiano-William-M.-Pack.pdf.

Carson, E. Ann, and William J. Sabol, *Aging of the State Prison Population, 1993–2013*. U.S Department of Justice, Bureau of Justice Statistics, May 2016, p.12. bjs.ojp.gov/content/pub/pdf/aspp9313.pdf.

Castro, Erin L., and Michael Brawn. "Critiquing Critical Pedagogies inside the Prison Classroom: A Dialogue between Student and Teacher." *Harvard Educational Review*, vol. 87, no. 1, 2017, pp. 99–121. doi:10.17763/1943-5045-87.1.99.

Cavallaro, Alexandra J., et al. "Inside Voices: Collaborative Writing in a Prison Environment." *Harlot: A Revealing Look at the Arts of Persuasion*, vol. 1, no.15, 2016, http://harlotofthearts.org/index.php/harlot/article/view/323/188.

Curry, Michelle, and Tobi Jacobi. "'Just Sitting in a Cell, You and Me': Sponsoring Writing in a County Jail." *Community Literacy Journal*, vol. 12, no. 1, 2017, pp. 5–22. doi:10.1353/clj.2017.0020.

Erby, Brandon M. "Imagining Freedom: Cultural Rhetorics, Digital Literacies, and Podcasting in Prison." *College Composition & Communication*, vol. 75, no. 1, Sept. 2023, pp. 224–41. doi:10.58680/ccc202332676.

Hutchinson, Glenn. "Detention/Writing Center Campaigns for Freedom." *Community Literacy Journal*, vol. 15, no. 1, Apr. 2021. doi:10.25148/CLJ.15.1.009362.

Jacobi, Tobi. "Against Infrastructure: Curating Community Literacy in a Jail Writing Program." *Community Literacy Journal*, vol. 11, no. 1, 2016, pp. 64–75, doi:10.25148/clj.11.1.009250.

Lewis, Rachel. "Troubling the Terms of Engagement: Queer Rhetorical Listening as Carceral Interruption." *Peitho: Journal of the Coalition of Feminist Scholars in the History of Rhetoric & Composition*, vol. 23, no. 1, Fall 2020, https://cfshrc.org/article/troubling-the-terms-of-engagement-queer-rhetorical-listening-as-carceral-interruption/.

Lockard, Joe, and Sherry Rankins-Robertson, editors. *Prison Pedagogies: Learning and Teaching with Imprisoned Writers*. Syracuse University Press, 2018.

McKillop, Matt, and Alex Boucher. "Aging Prison Populations Drive up Costs." *The Pew Charitable Trusts*, The Pew Charitable Trusts, 20 Feb. 2018, www.pewtrusts.org/en/research-and-analysis/articles/2018/02/20/aging-prison-populations-drive-up-costs.

Middleton, Logan. "Prison Pedagogies of Place: Leveraging Space, Time, and Institutional Knowledge in Higher Education in Prison Teaching." *Journal of Higher Education in Prison*, vol. 2, no. 1, pp. 100-119, https://assets-global.website-files.com/5e3dd3cf0b4b54470c8b1be1/6490c4f7612858e229993798_JHEP_V2_Middleton.pdf.

Plemons, Anna. *Beyond Progress in the Prison Classroom: Options and Opportunities*. National Council of Teachers of English, 2019.

Novotny, Maria and John T. Gagnon. "Research as Care: A Shared Ownership Approach to Rhetorical Research in Trauma Communities." *Reflections: A Journal of Public Rhetoric, Civic Writing and Service Learning*, vol. 18, no. (1), pp. 71-101.

Novotny, Maria, et al. "Community-Driven Concepts to Support TPC Coalition Building in a Post- *Roe* World." *Communication Design Quarterly*, vol. 11, no. 2, July 2023, pp. 28–37. doi:10.1145/3592356.3592360.

Rogers, Laura. "Keywords: Prison." *Community Literacy Journal*, vol. 6, no. 2, Apr. 2012. doi:10.25148/CLJ.6.2.009399.

"Sex Offender Registration and Notification Act (SORNA)." *The United States Department of Justice*, 15 Aug. 2022, www.justice.gov/criminal-ceos/sex-offender-registration-and-notification-act-sorna.

Author Bios

David Kocik is a PhD candidate in English: Media, Cinema and Digital Studies at the University of Wisconsin-Milwaukee. His academic work focuses on the intersections of pedagogy, games, and digital media, and he has extensive experience developing instructor training programs and curriculum for first year composition courses.

Kayla Fettig is a graduate student in the Public Rhetoric and Community Engagement program at the University of Wisconsin-Milwaukee. She is the graduate representative for CCCC's, contributing newsletter writer for the re-entry non-profit organization The Community, and is passionate about disabled students and accessibility in first year composition classrooms.

Maria Novotny is an Associate Professor of English at the University of Wisconsin-Milwaukee where she teaches in the Rhetoric, Professional Writing, and Community Engagement graduate program. She also serves as a member of the Program Committee for the Coalition of Community Writing.

Casey O'Ceallaigh is an Assistant Professor of English at Mount Mary University. They received their PhD from the University of Wisconsin-Milwaukee where their work focused on using multimodal methods to create an inclusive classroom.

Book and New Media Reviews

From the Book and New Media Review Editor's Desk

Jessica Shumake, Editor
University of Notre Dame

In Louise Erdrich's book *The Blue Jay's Dance*, she describes looking through plant and seed catalogues in the dead of winter. "The pictures vanquish the frozen monotony and calm me, but of course they also exceed the reality of what will, in truth, turn out to be my garden" (Erdrich 33). Erdrich continues that the garden beds raised in one's imagination during the darkest days of winter—and tended during summer months—are places of the spirit where she goes when the winds howl. It's sustaining to breathe in the knowledge that there's at least one cold-hardy clump of wild ferns in my yard that "in secluded lightlessness," unknown and unforced, is facing winter with the resolve of a survivor (Erdrich 37).

The two reviews in this section are as welcome as spring fiddleheads unfurling in my yard in Northern Indiana. I'm grateful to Rosanne Carlo and Patrick Thomas Morgan for their beautiful writing and hope their reviews sustain *CLJ* readers' imaginations and enliven community-engaged writing spaces.

Works Cited

Erdrich, Louise. *The Blue Jay's Dance: A Memoir of Early Motherhood*. Harper Perennial, 2010.

The Writing of Where: Graffiti and the Production of Writing Spaces

Charles N. Lesh
Syracuse University P, 2022, 304 pp.

Reviewed by Rosanne Carlo
College of Staten Island (CUNY)

Charles N. Lesh

The Writing of Where

Graffiti and the Production of Writing Spaces

Charles Lesh's book, *The Writing of Where: Graffiti and The Production of Writing Spaces,* challenges mainstream notions in the field of writing studies, such as the definition of public writing, what "counts" as writing, and who is a writer. His ethnographic method, interviewing graffiti writers in Boston and participating in the creation of writing spaces with them, offers a model for community-based research that centers reciprocity. Lesh claims the book as a space that "calls forth a public and a consequent set of values in relation to the ethos of community partnerships in rhetoric and composition" (25). To me, this is why the book is an important read and contribution to community writing.

Lesh focuses on the importance of place and writing, specifically on the city of Boston, documenting its history of hostility to graffiti, and its writers, as a way of analyzing a counterpublic that is thriving and working to rewrite the city's normative script. He discusses Boston's conservatism through tracing narratives of its Puritanical founding and its obsession in memorializing its own history as well as its development today into a gentrified, neoliberal city. "Boston is like your old grandmother that you're just waiting to croak because she just won't give up those old ways" (80), graffiti writer TENSE observes. Perhaps, too, writing studies is like your old grandmother—dictating to scholar-teachers what methods we should use, what counts as writing or publics or community, and what aims we should strive for in our scholarly work. Disciplinarity can be an inscribed circle of naming what we know. Though Lesh's book does value classical rhetorical concepts at the center of writing studies, such as invention, style, delivery (à la circulation), and ethos, he also pushes readers forward to imagine writing outside traditional institutional spaces and genres.

The "wheres" of writing is explicitly tied to invention, and graffiti writers are on the cutting edge of that process of production: "Graffiti writers make space, sure, in a general sense. But, what's more, they make *spots,* they make *bibles,* they make *trains.*

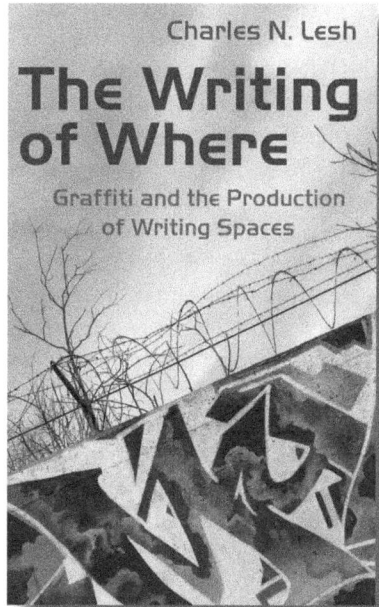

They make new publics and new *wheres* of public writing" (20). Through analyzing the practices, products, and circulation of graffiti writers' work, Lesh argues that writing studies can learn a thing or two about how to produce itself in a more capacious and inclusive way.

Lesh helps readers understand the art of graffiti—that it is a form of writing and that the artists identify as writers—in this sense, he identifies a gap in our disciplinary understandings of what counts as "writing," which overlooks graffiti. As a New Yorker, graffiti is everywhere in my life—on the rooftops of the Brooklyn-Queens Expressway (BQE), on the railroad trellises and underpasses of the Metro North line, on the skate park ramps in my South Brooklyn neighborhood, on the trains in the freight yard by the Owls Head Wastewater Treatment Plant, in the bathroom stalls in the ladies' room at College of Staten Island (CSI). After I read Lesh's book, the graffiti that was always there became more visible, more meaningful to me. I started to think about the writers and why they wrote. I could better "read" graffiti, understand the labor and processes of its writers, and also see it as an art and as a way of remaking—or speaking back to—the official discourses of a city. But, graffiti isn't just for us city folk. It's also for people far and wide. Its circulation, particularly via freight trains, allows us to view graffiti as it moves across the country, even in Lesh's new "where" of Opelika, Alabama (229).

The introduction, and the "Community Interludes" sections, feature the voices of the graffiti writers Lesh created with; they offer insights into their identities as writers and their writing practices. The reputation of a graffiti writer is built up over time and place, practicing their developing styles on blackbooks (also called bibles) and walls as well as in the circulation of their pieces. A graffiti writer has an ethos. This idea of ethos hit home for me when I read LIFE's words: " . . . Something about me feels proud when I say I am a writer. Because I am writing mostly based in letters. It all came from writing your name. This is who I am and I am going to say it. I just think of a writer as fucking someone who really knows their shit. They know their history. They know the writers before them. They know their city's history. They know the ropes. They know the etiquette" (28). Immediately, this reflection from LIFE reminded me of Michael Halloran's definition of ethos, which is a concept not only meant in personal terms but also in a community and place-based way. You don't just write for yourself, you write to show and reflect your membership in a community. Halloran expands: "The most concrete meaning given for the term in the Greek lexicon is 'a habitual gathering place,' and I suspect that it is upon this image of people gathering together in a public place, sharing experiences and ideas, that its meaning as character rests. To have ethos is to manifest the virtues most valued by the culture to and for which one speaks" (60). In other words, to have ethos is to know your shit and your history and your city.

Lesh is concerned about ethos because he wants to be seen as part of the public of graffiti writers and not just academically analyzing them. This is essential in developing the spatial concept of reciprocity Lesh models in the book (223). So, Lesh participates in the Boston culture of graffiti by frequenting places of significance, such as the Kulturez writing space and The Lab, as well as indexing his work in a blackbook (or bible). Additionally, Lesh serves as someone who participates in the actual production of graffiti, in the legal space of the warehouse in Quincy, MA, but also illegal places. Lesh describes being out on walks with other artists returning to or creating new spots for graffiti. On one such trip, he is assisting writer NIRO: "I clear beer bottles and other highway trash and sit in a position where I can see the wall, the highway, and the parking lot. My role tonight is lookout. As NIRO fills in the R, a state trooper drives by. "'Yo, down,' I whisper, and we both get low" (89). In this description, the "where" of graffiti is featured. The writers are distinctive individuals in this, Lesh being among them, but they are building and reflecting a culture and a history; they are a public.

In chapter one, "Boston(s)," Lesh indexes the ways Boston outlaws difference, and graffiti writers, through its culture and laws. He indexes "the dominant literacy landscapes" of Boston to contrast these with the potential new scripts the writers create on this old text (Lesh 34). Lesh ties Boston to the idea of the Melting Pot, or a belief in assimilation and eradication of difference; to its role as The Athens of America, in being a place with many universities and a highly, traditionally educated citizenry; to its preservation of history as a Cradle of Liberty, evidenced by its many monuments and sacred spaces—a version of "product not process" (52); and, finally, its present, gentrifying state, New Boston, where graffiti needs to be buffed to make way for neoliberal visions of grayness and profit. The important concept to take away from this chapter is how the practice of graffiti, and the bodies of the writers themselves, are othered and criminalized in Boston. The writers are of someplace else, not part of the official writing of the city. Lesh argues that this is all the more reason to understand and read graffiti writing, because ". . . it is in this very place-less-ness that allows us to uncover something about the rhetorical politics of the city more generally: what writing is welcome, what writers are welcome, and how identities of the city are constantly being produced and reinforced through writing" (65). Through studying graffiti writers and their practices, we are looking into the "wheres" outside of dominant spaces and discourses.

In chapter two, "Spot," Lesh defines the public places of graffiti as "spatial ecologies" that are created by the graffiti-writing public and serve as "writing spaces" to communicate and develop community practice (87). Spots are created through attunement to the city, through walking, through understanding the politics of where, through seeing spots where your writing can exist and be seen by others. Spots, both legal and illegal, are spaces where graffiti writing can exist and change the city script. Graffiti writers use sensemaking in their practice (96). One graffiti writer, VISE, explains this ability to see spots everywhere as he became further enmeshed in his craft: "[Graffiti] made me look at my environment differently and to find opportunities to express myself creatively in everything. Every thing, every space, has potential for creativity, to be changed" (Lesh 76). Additionally, the development of "chill" spots, where multiple writers add their pieces, tags, and throwups, creates spaces for a kind of pedagogical "reading" of the style and encourages imitation and invention. This is a form of genre theory, as writers learn the expectations and histories of their community: "That is, writers themselves, in pedagogical spaces of their own making, construct and learn systems of uptake that organize texts hierarchically and meticulously, in ways that deviate dramatically from the rules that govern the naming of space in New Boston" (Lesh 110).

In chapter three, "Bible," Lesh talks about the graffiti writer's practice of keeping a blackbook in which they practice their lettering and style as well as exchange them with others. The blackbook, or bible as they call it in Boston, is viewed as talismanic (135) and imbued with a quality that is at once private and public writing (131), but additionally, not the kind of production that is meant for sale or consumption in a marketplace (161). In this way, bibles are a community and pedagogical space, where writing circulates and travels across pages, space, and time. Graffiti writers TENSE and HATE both equate the bible to a place where the style of the writer is developed; it is a record of their evolving style (135, 139). Lesh further discusses the blackbook in pedagogical terms. Writer MYND gives Lesh some feedback on how to write the "CH" lettering in his name, telling him he can "run with it." Lesh reflects on this experience as being not far from the practices of feedback and assessment in writing studies: "Hanging out at the shop, flipping through bibles, critiquing and revising texts were the most common activities of this study. It's also a scene that feels familiar to me as a teacher of writing. . . A first draft, a collaborative workshop, a revision. There's writing pedagogy here in this community space" (137).

In chapter four, "Trains," Lesh discusses how graffiti on trains is related to writing circulation and its ability to be seen: "Trains give writers a stable infrastructure for circulation to audiences near and far, affiliated and unaffiliated, interested and hostile" (178). Lesh's discussion of trains goes back to the NYC subways of the 70s and 80s and how the visual ways messages were carried throughout the city and worked to go against the normative, neoliberal script of the city—the aesthetics of Walter Hill's film *The Warriors* (1979) comes to mind here. The graffiti culture of NYC trains inspired Boston writers as LIFE describes going to NYC as a "tour" where the trains provided, "nuggets of inspiration, these nuggets of how to do it, where to do it, and who is doing it" (201). The idea of the train is at once nostalgic, tied to graffiti's roots (TEMP 211), and also future-oriented as graffiti writers envision their writings existing in other locales and times beyond the moment of creation (BEAN 212). Finally, this chapter and the following interlude define an important concept of graffiti, *benching*, where writers sit and observe trains to learn more about style—again, very relevant to the idea of the pedagogy of graffiti writing. Graffiti writer TEMP best describes this practice of benching on his trip to NYC: "Man, that's all I did when I went there. My friend got bored with me. I just wanted to absorb style. I went to the Grand Concourse station and sat on those benches. That is where you could go see style. That was like a museum for graffiti style, on and around those trains" (209).

In the final chapter five, "Warehouse," Lesh discusses his methodology for the book and his hopes for what it might provide for the field of community writing. Lesh identifies this wing of the field as being the "most explicitly dedicated to rhetorical spaciousness, to cultivating robust rhetorical landscapes within and beyond the academy, and to pushing the boundary of where writing (studies) is and what writing (studies) can do" (233). Lesh's book on Boston graffiti examines a public that is creating new "wheres" of writing, and therefore, rewriting the script of Boston to be ". . . a more dynamic and equitable city, one where more voices are present and different orientation to city life are announced" (220). We can learn from the graffiti writers' practices and try to envision writing studies as having a different orientation to knowledge and writing, one that is more dynamic and equitable.

Works Cited

Halloran, Michael S. "Aristotle's Concept of Ethos, or If Not His Somebody Else's." *Rhetoric Review.* vol. 1, no. 1, 1982, 58–63.

Violent Exceptions: Children's Human Rights and Humanitarian Rhetorics

Wendy S. Hesford
Ohio State UP, 2021, 260 pp.

Reviewed by Patrick Thomas Morgan
University of Louisiana Monroe

T he tragedy of this book is that it is always relevant: we are continually presented with emergencies that require the keen tools Wendy S. Hesford uses in *Violent Exceptions: Children's Human Rights and Humanitarian Rhetorics*. In this cogent and timely study, Hesford focuses on the figure of the child-in-peril. These are the faces that circulate in news media after catastrophes. Charities depict them to raise money. Politicians invoke their memories to justify policies. Portrayals of imperiled children are powerful humanitarian arguments, coalescing complex, systemic cruelties in the immediacy of embodied innocence. It is precisely this clash between two different chronologies—the systemic and the immediate—that Hesford so expertly unpacks.

When you think of the child-in-peril, what image comes to mind? Hesford's first instance involves ICE detention facilities in Texas. The book's examples multiply with each chapter. There's the Flint water crisis, embodied by the bruise-like rashes covering the face of Sincere Smith on the cover of *Time* magazine. Or the shell-shocked stare and bloodied face of Omran Daqneesh, sitting in an ambulance after the bombing of Aleppo. Or the body of Alan Kurdi lying facedown on a Turkish beach after attempting to escape the Syrian civil war by boat and drowning in the Mediterranean Sea. As I write this review, the Russian invasion has displaced millions of Ukrainian children, and their stories and images are being used for multiple purposes. Who determines what these figurations of the child-in-peril mean? Why does *this* image signify *this* event? How do we unpack how the depictions circulate through various media, and what is at stake? What kinds of power dynamics do these images reveal, and what do they obscure? These are just a few of the compelling questions Hesford's book invites.

One of the key conceptual tools in this study—the origin of its analytic energy—comes from the contrast between human rights and humanitarianism. These two concepts work within distinct temporalities. Human rights tend to work in lon-

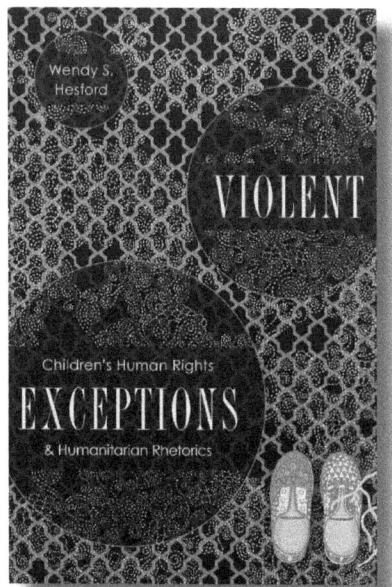

ger frameworks and emphasize agency. Humanitarianism works in shorter frameworks and emphasizes passivity. Thus we have a central problem when the figure of the child-in-peril and children's human rights are framed from a humanitarian viewpoint. As Hesford argues, humanitarian frameworks can serve as tools for distraction, focusing attention on the immediate emergency rather than the long-term, systemic patterns that cause the emergency. Humanitarian frameworks, in other words, can characterize a tragedy as an exception when it is the natural outgrowth of national and international policies. The major argument and illumination of Hesford's manuscript explore this central paradox: "how the iconic figure of the child-in-peril erases slow violence—the violence of the ordinary—from which the spectacle of the imperiled child emerges" (20).

Hesford's argument is applied to five rhetorical case studies, analyzing child refugees, child humanitarian celebrities, disabled African child soldiers, African American children and carceral systems, and transgender and intersex children. Drawing on the interdisciplinary work of new materialism, Hesford examines the child-in-peril figure using "material rhetoric," foregrounding "the material and discursive as co-constitutive" (22). Alongside material rhetoric, Hesford uses a genealogical approach, which "focuses on the discursive and material practices through which truths and nontruths or exceptions are constructed" (24). These two methodologies blend well together. In the classroom, professors could assign one of Hesford's case studies to understand her methodology and apply this material-genealogical approach to new scenarios. Readers interested in visual rhetoric and how images circulate in culture will find this book particularly illuminating.

The first chapter focuses on the mediation of child refugee images, from the Syrian civil war to the US-Mexico border, and how arguments build around images to elicit action, conveying the idea that a threshold has been crossed. Two iconic images this chapter analyzes include those of Omran Daqneesh and Alan Kurdi. Hesford points out how, for Syrians trying to flee by boat over the Mediterranean Sea, the sea is technically an option because it is a "free zone," and yet "states monitor navigation and control maritime resources" to such an extent that the journey becomes perilous (58). These images of refugee children-in-peril, mobilized to elicit humanitarian reactions, illustrate a fundamental contradiction: "turning the refugee crisis into a humanitarian matter fails to recognize the problem as a political crisis caused by geopolitics and by economic, legal, and environmental injustices on a global scale" (58). Well intentioned as it is, humanitarianism, according to Hesford, nevertheless places its subjects within a frame of passivity, always the victim in need of rescue and never the agent fighting for rights.

This first chapter also exemplifies an organizing structure Hesford uses throughout that eschews overly centralized, linear argumentation in favor of what she calls a "metastructure of juxtaposition," in which she places cases side-by-side and implicitly invites the reader to become an active interpreter of the texts (30). In this way, the book embodies its own argument insofar as it encourages interpretive agency over passivity. This juxtaposition structure leads to chapters with a wide variety of texts, such as the following in the first chapter alone: journalism, photography, speech, art exhibition, documentary film, memoir, and poetry. Indeed, the juxtaposition structure is so effective at drawing in the reader, inviting analysis, that one feels compelled to pause and study the various examples. For example, after the concrete details of a memoir written by Tima Kurdi—Alan Kurdi's aunt—the book juxtaposes a long excerpt from Khaled Hosseini's *Sea Prayer*.

Inspired by Alan Kurdi's story, the poem consists of a father's words to his sleeping son the night before an attempted crossing of the Mediterranean Sea. Hesford includes it to show both the limits and rhetorical power of humanitarian frameworks, as the poem poignantly portrays the father's powerlessness, and yet reframes "denigrating taxonomies through the egalitarian ideal of universal humanity" (59). On closer inspection, the excerpt manifests this reframing in multiple ways. The poem declares the refugees' precarity by dividing the space of the poem along two axes: the horizontal travel that means survival versus the narrator's overriding thought of nature's depths: "how deep the sea, / and how vast, how indifferent. / How powerless I am to protect you from it" (59). The system is set up to travel vertically—downward, to death—in a world where survival depends on the horizontal. Prayer becomes the one means of re-inscribing value in a space that devalues life, as the following line transitions the poem from thought to action in a one-line stanza: "All I can do is pray" (59). It's as if this solitary line, amidst longer stanzas, embodies the sense of helplessness: a string of words lost amidst a sea of adversity. He prays that "God steers the vessel true" when the boat is far from land "and we are a flyspeck / in the heaving waters, pitching and tilting" (59). He declares that his son Marwan is "precious cargo," and prays "the sea knows this" (59). The clash of meaning between the words "flyspeck" and "precious" further illustrates the radically divergent value systems between his petitionary prayer and the material realities of the sea crossing. There's a glimmer of hope as the poem embraces the collective pronoun "we"—as if they are going to make it out alive—but quickly fragments into "you" and "I" with the jarring disparity between the words "precious" and "cargo." "Cargo" is an objectifying word, a nod to the larger political and economic forces that created the situation. This is a poem that starkly dramatizes the power differences that lie at the heart of the book. By ending the poem with a line earnestly praying that "the sea knows this" (i.e. how precious Marwan is), the paternal narrator implies that the poem is working in two frames: the sea is both the materially specific Mediterranean Sea and also a stand-in for any reader who likewise must be converted—via the humanitarian framework—from indifference to knowledge. In his prayer, the sea transforms from a chaotic other to an entity capable of grasping the value of human life. The tragedy is that we already know how the story ends.

Throughout the rest of the book, each case study attentively elaborates—in examples just as striking as the preceding poem—upon the contrast between humanitarian and human rights frameworks. The second chapter shows how women impacted by Islamic terrorism, such as Malala Yousafzai, are transformed from victims into politically passive humanitarian celebrities. Hesford contends that media's focus on these exceptional female figures commodifies them in the end, and this commercialization acts as a smokescreen for the political situation causing suffering in the first place.

According to Hesford, "media, government, and corporate stakeholders have tamed Malala's rhetoric by translating her resistance into stock neoliberal narratives of girl empowerment" (99). The third chapter, focusing on disabled African child soldiers, argues that an international focus on human rights violations distracts from domestic violations. Hesford shows how the resilience of child amputees becomes a useful narrative allowing the powerful to once again frame "systemic problems and injustices as isolated emergencies" (132). This chapter focuses in particular on the prosthesis, which becomes more than the physicality of a limb replacement, and more of a symbol of humanitarianism's politically neutralizing intervention. As Hesford writes, "within the neoliberal humanitarian imaginary, the Sierra Leone child amputee's lost limb is configured as a 'negative space, a space of absence' that calls for the presence and 'gifting' of Western humanity and futurity" (123-124).

The fourth chapter analyzes how racialized state violence places African American children outside the category of child. Think Trayvon Martin and the way, as his story circulated through the media, his identity narrowed such that he was denied "the legal status of child" (154). As Hesford elaborates, "Focusing on humanitarian negations of the human rights of Black children and the consequences of these negations for Black communities in the US, this chapter exposes the political limitations of the humanitarian paradigm of human rights recognition for addressing systemic inequities arising from racial capitalism" (140). The fifth chapter examines how humanitarianism frames queer children's rights as "exceptional, even when the circumstances that condition these rights violations are systemic and everyday" (172). Analyzing three documentary films—*Growing Up Coy* (2016), *Getting Out* (2011), and *She's Not a Boy* (2019)—to better understand the withholding of children's rights, Hesford analyzes what she calls "the optics of *queer liminality*" (171). This term refers to "the in-between spaces and identities that challenge the stability of the heteronormative gender binaries that undergird the tolerance threshold and its figuration of the child-in-peril" (171).

Overall, these five case studies capture the dynamism of intersecting power structures as images circulate through culture, positioned by different entities for different ends. Although primarily useful for rhetoric, communication, and human rights scholars, Hesford's materialist methodology and wide range of case studies make the book valuable for community-engaged writing studies scholars and other scholarly approaches, such as feminist, disability, childhood, literacy, and literary studies.

PARLOR PRESS

EQUIPMENT FOR LIVING

Now with Parlor Press!

Studies in Rhetorics and Feminism
New Series Editors: Jessica Enoch and Sharon Yam

Emerging Conversations in the Global Humanities
Series Editor: Victor E. Taylor

New Releases

Writing Proposals and Grants 3e by Richard Johnson-Sheehan and Paul Thompson Hunter

Rhetorics of Evidence: Science – Media – Culture edited by edited by Olaf Kramer and Michael Pelzer

Kenneth Burke's Rhetoric of Identification by Tilly Warnock

The Forever Colony by Victor Villanueva

Keywords in Making edited by Jason Tham

Inclusive Aims: Rhetoric's Role in Reproductive Justice edited by Heather Brook Adams and Nancy Myers

Not Playing Around: Feminist and Queer Rhetorics in Videogames by Rebecca Richards

Design for Composition: Inspiration for Creative Visual and Multimodal Projects by Sohui Lee and Russell Carpenter

MLA Mina Shaughnessy Prize and CCCC Best Book Award 2021!

Creole Composition: Academic Writing and Rhetoric in the Anglophone Caribbean, edited by Vivette Milson-Whyte, Raymond Oenbring, and Brianne Jaquette

Check Out Our Website!

Discounts, blog, open access titles, instant downloads, and more.

www.parlorpress.com

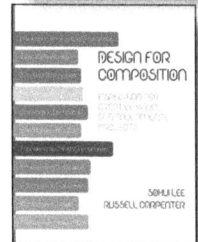

CLJ **Discount:** Use CLJ20 at checkout to receive a 20% discount on all titles not on sale through November 1, 2024.

Milton Keynes UK
Ingram Content Group UK Ltd.
UKHW041835201024
449814UK00004B/421

9 781643 174938